THE FIGHT FOR A FREE SEA

EXTRA-ILLUSTRATED EDITION

∵

VOLUME 17
THE CHRONICLES
OF AMERICA SERIES
ALLEN JOHNSON
EDITOR

GERHARD R. LOMER
CHARLES W. JEFFERYS
ASSISTANT EDITORS

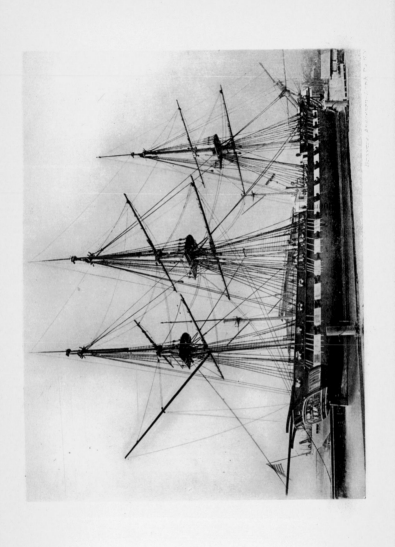

"OLD IRONSIDES"

The old frigate *Constitution* as she appears today in her snug berth at the Boston Navy Yard where she is preserved as an historical relic.

Photograph by N. L. Stebbins, Boston.

THE FIGHT FOR A FREE SEA

A CHRONICLE OF THE
WAR OF 1812
BY RALPH D. PAINE

NEW HAVEN: YALE UNIVERSITY PRESS
TORONTO: GLASGOW, BROOK & CO.
LONDON: HUMPHREY MILFORD
OXFORD UNIVERSITY PRESS

CONTENTS

ILLUSTRATIONS

ix

THE FIGHT FOR A FREE SEA

∵

CHAPTER I

"ON TO CANADA!"

THE American people of today, weighed in the balances of the greatest armed conflict of all time and found not wanting, can afford to survey, in a spirit of candid scrutiny and without reviving an ancient grudge, that turbulent episode in the welding of their nation which is called the War of 1812. In spite of defeats and disappointments this war was, in the large, enduring sense, a victory. It was in this renewed defiance of England that the dream of the founders of the Republic and the ideals of the embattled farmers of Bunker Hill and Saratoga achieved their goal. Henceforth the world was to respect these States, not as so many colonies bitterly wrangling among themselves, but as a sovereign and independent nation.

1

The War of 1812, like the American Revolution, was a valiant contest for survival on the part of the spirit of freedom.   It was essentially akin to the world-wide struggle of a century later, when sons of the old foemen of 1812 — sons of the painted Indians and of the Kentucky pioneers in fringed buckskins, sons of the New Hampshire ploughboys clad in homespun, sons of the Canadian militia and the red-coated regulars of the British line, sons of the tarry seamen of the *Constitution* and the *Guerrière* — stood side by side as brothers in arms to save from brutal obliteration the same spirit of freedom.   And so it is that in Flanders fields today the poppies blow above the graves of the sons of the men who fought each other a century ago in the Michigan wilderness and at Lundy's Lane.

The causes and the background of the War of 1812 are presented elsewhere in this series of Chronicles.[1]   Great Britain, at death grips with Napoleon, paid small heed to the rights and dignities of neutral nations.   The harsh and selfish maritime policy of the age, expressed in the British Navigation Acts and intensified by the struggle with Napoleon, led the Mistress of the Seas to perpetrate

[1] See *Jefferson and His Colleagues*, by Allen Johnson (in *The Chronicles of America*).

indignity after indignity on the ships and sailors which were carrying American commerce around the world. The United States demanded a free sea, which Great Britain would not grant. Of necessity, then, such futile weapons as embargoes and non-intercourse acts had to give place to the musket, the bayonet, and the carronade. There could be no compromise between the clash of doctrines. It was for the United States to assert herself, regardless of the odds, or sink into a position of supine dependency upon the will of Great Britain and the wooden walls of her invincible navy. "Free Trade and Sailors' Rights!" was the American war cry. It expressed the two grievances which outweighed all others — the interference with American shipping and the ruthless impressment of seamen from beneath the Stars and Stripes. No less high-handed than Great Britain's were Napoleon's offenses against American commerce, and there was just cause for war with France. Yet Americans felt the greater enmity toward England, partly as an inheritance from the Revolution, but chiefly because of the greater injury which England had wrought, owing to her superior strength on the sea.

There were, to be sure, other motives in the conflict. It is not to be supposed that the frontiersmen of the Northwest and Southwest, who hailed the war with enthusiasm, were ardently aroused to redress wrongs inflicted upon their seafaring countrymen. Their enmity towards Great Britain was compounded of quite different grievances. Behind the recent Indian wars on the frontier they saw, or thought they saw, British paymasters. The red trappers and hunters of the forest were bloodily defending their lands; and there was a long-standing bond of interest between them and the British in Canada. The British were known to the tribes generally as fur traders, not "land stealers"; and the great traffic carried on by the merchants of Montreal, not only in the Canadian wilderness but also in the American Northwest, naturally drew Canadians and Indians into the same camp. "On to Canada!" was the slogan of the frontiersmen. It expressed at once their desire to punish the hereditary foe and to rid themselves of an unfriendly power to the north.

The United States was poorly prepared and equipped for military and naval campaigns when, in June, 1812, Congress declared war on Great Britain. Nothing had been learned from the costly blunders of the Revolution, and the delusion that readiness for war was a menace to democracy had influenced the Government to absurd extremes. The regular army comprised only sixty-seven hundred men, scattered over an enormous country and on garrison service from which they could not be safely withdrawn. They were without traditions and without experience in actual warfare. Winfield Scott, at that time a young officer in the regular army, wrote:

The old officers had very generally sunk into either sloth, ignorance, or habits of intemperate drinking. . . . Many of the appointments were positively bad, and a majority of the remainder indifferent. Party spirit of that day knew no bounds, and was of course blind to policy. Federalists were almost entirely excluded from selection, though great numbers were eager for the field. . . . Where there was no lack of educated men in the dominant party, the appointments consisted generally of swaggerers, dependents, decayed gentlemen, and others "fit for nothing else," which always turned out utterly unfit for any military purpose whatever.

The main reliance was to be on militia and volunteers, an army of the free people rushing to arms in defense of their liberties, as voiced by Jefferson and echoed more than a century later by another spokesman of democracy. There was the stuff for splendid soldiers in these farmers and woodsmen, but in many lamentable instances their regiments were no more than irresponsible armed mobs.   Until as recently as the War with Spain, the perilous fallacy persisted that the States should retain control of their several militia forces in time of war and deny final authority to the Federal Government.   It was this doctrine which so nearly wrecked the cause of the Revolution.   George Washington had learned the lesson through painful experience, but his counsel was wholly disregarded; and, because it serves as a text and an interpretation for much of the humiliating history which we are about to follow, that counsel is here quoted in part. Washington wrote in retrospect:

Had we formed a permanent army in the beginning. which by the continuance of the same men in service had been capable of discipline, we never should have had to retreat with a handful of men across the Delaware in 1776, trembling for the fate of America, which nothing but the infatuation of the enemy could have saved; we should not have remained all the succeeding winter at their mercy, with sometimes scarcely a sufficient body of men to mount the ordinary guards, liable at every moment to be dissipated if they had only thought proper to march against us; we should not have been under the necessity of fighting Brandywine with an unequal number of raw troops, and afterwards of seeing Philadelphia fall a prey to a victorious army; we should not have been at Valley Forge with less than half the force of the enemy, destitute of everything, in a situation neither to resist or to retire; we should not have seen New York left with a handful of men, yet an overmatch for the main army of these States, while the principal part of their force was detached for the reduction of two of them; we should not have found ourselves this spring so weak as to be insulted by 5000 men, unable to protect our baggage and magazines, their security depending on a good countenance and a want of enterprise in the enemy; we should not have been, the greatest part of the war, inferior to the enemy, indebted for our safety to their inactivity, enduring frequently the mortification of seeing inviting opportunities to ruin them pass unimproved for want of a force which the country was completely able to afford, and of seeing the country ravaged, our towns burnt, the inhabitants plundered, abused, murdered, with impunity from the same cause.

The War of 1812, besides being hampered by short enlistments, confused authority, and incompetent officers, was fought by a country and an army divided against itself. When Congress authorized the enrollment of one hundred thousand militia, the governors of Massachusetts and Connecticut refused to furnish their quotas, objecting to the command of United States officers and to the sending of men beyond the borders of their own States. This attitude fairly indicated the feeling of New England, which was opposed to the war and openly spoke of secession.   Moreover, the wealthy merchants and bankers of New England declined to subscribe to the national loans when the Treasury at Washington was bankrupt, and vast quantities of supplies were shipped from New England seaports to the enemy in Canada.   It was an extraordinary paradox that those States which had seen their sailors impressed by thousands and which had suffered most heavily from England's attacks on neutral commerce should have arrayed themselves in bitter opposition to the cause and the Government.   It was "Mr. Madison's War," they said, and he could win or lose it — and pay the bills, for that matter.

The American navy was in little better plight than the army.   England flew the royal ensign over six hundred ships of war and was the undisputed sovereign of the seas.   Opposed to this mighty armada were five frigates, three ships, and seven brigs, which Monroe recommended should be "kept in a body in a safe port."   Not worth mention were the two hundred ridiculous little gunboats which had to stow the one cannon below to prevent capsizing when they ventured out of harbor.   These craft were a pet notion of Jefferson.   "Believing, myself," he said of them, "that gunboats are the only water defense which can be useful to us and protect us from the ruinous folly of a navy, I am pleased with everything which promises to improve them."

A nation of eight million people, unready, blundering, rent by internal dissension, had resolved to challenge an England hardened by war and tremendously superior in military resources. It was not all madness, however, for the vast empire of Canada lay exposed to invasion, and in this quarter the enemy was singularly vulnerable. Henry Clay spoke for most of his countrymen beyond the boundaries of New England when he announced to Congress: "The conquest of Canada is in your power. I trust that I shall not be deemed presumptuous when I state that I verily believe that the militia of Kentucky are alone competent to place Montreal and Upper Canada at your feet. Is it nothing to the British nation; is it nothing to the pride of her monarch to have the last immense North American possession held by him in the commencement of his reign wrested from his dominions?" Even Jefferson was deluded into predicting that the capture of Canada as far as Quebec would be a mere matter of marching through the country and would give the troops experience for the attack on Halifax and the final expulsion of England from the American continent.

The British Provinces, extending twelve hundred miles westward to Lake Superior, had a population of less than five hundred thousand; but a third of these were English immigrants or American Loyalists and their descendants, types of folk who would hardly sit idly and await invasion. That they should resist or strike back seems not to have been expected in the war councils of the amiable Mr. Madison. Nor were other and manifold dangers taken into account by those who counseled war. The Great Lakes were defenseless, the warlike Indians of the Northwest were in arms and awaiting the British summons, while the whole country beyond the Wabash and the Maumee was almost unguarded. Isolated here and there were stockades containing a few dozen men beyond hope of rescue, frontier posts of what is now the Middle West. Plans of campaign were prepared without thought of the insuperable difficulties of transport through regions in which there were neither roads, provisions, towns, nor navigable rivers. Armies were maneuvered and victories won upon the maps in the office of the Secretary of War. Generals were selected by some inscrutable process which decreed that dull-witted, pompous incapables should bungle campaigns and waste lives.

It was wisely agreed that of all the strategic points along this far-flung and thinly held frontier, Detroit should receive the earliest attention. At all costs this point was to be safeguarded as a base for the advance into Canada from the west. A remote trading post within gunshot of the enemy across the river and menaced by tribes of hostile Indians, Detroit then numbered eight hundred inhabitants and was protected only by a stout enclosure of logs. For two hundred miles to the nearest friendly settlements in Ohio, the line of communications was a forest trail which skirted Lake Erie for some distance and could easily be cut by the enemy. From Detroit it was the intention of the Americans to strike the first blow at the Canadian post of Amherstburg near by.

The stage was now set for the entrance of General William Hull as one of the luckless, unheroic figures upon whom the presidential power of appointment bestowed the trappings of high military command. He was by no means the worst of these. In fact, the choice seemed auspicious. Hull had seen honorable service in the Revolution and had won the esteem of George Washington.

He was now Governor of Michigan Territory. At sixty years of age he had no desire to gird on the sword.   He was persuaded by Madison, however, to accept a brigadier general's commission and to lead the force ordered to Detroit. His instructions were vague, but in June, 1812, shortly before the declaration of war, he took command of two thousand regulars and militia at Dayton, Ohio, and began the arduous advance through the wilderness towards Detroit. The adventure was launched with energy. These hardy, reliant men knew how to cut roads, to bridge streams, and to exist on scanty rations. Until sickness began to decimate their ranks, they advanced at an encouraging rate and were almost halfway to Detroit when the tidings of the outbreak of hostilities overtook them.

General Hull forthwith hurried his troops to the Maumee River, leaving their camp equipment and heavy stores behind.   He now committed his first crass blunder. Though the British controlled the waters of Lake Erie, yet he sent a schooner ahead with all his hospital supplies, intrenching tools, official papers, and muster rolls. The little vessel was captured within sight of Detroit and the documents proved invaluable to the British commander of Upper Canada, Major General Isaac Brock, who gained thereby a complete idea of the American plans and proceeded to act accordingly. Brock was a soldier of uncommon intelligence and resolution, acquitting himself with distinction, and contrasting with his American adversaries in a manner rather painful to contemplate.

At length Hull reached Detroit and crossed the river to assume the offensive. He was strongly hopeful of success. The Canadians appeared friendly and several hundred sought his protection. Even the enemy's militia were deserting to his colors. In a proclamation Hull looked forward to a bloodless conquest, informing the Canadians that they were to be emancipated from tyranny and oppression and restored to the dignified station of freemen. "I have a force which will break down all opposition," said he, "and that force is but the vanguard of a much greater."

He soundly reasoned that unless a movement could be launched against Niagara, at the other end of Lake Erie, the whole strength of the British might be thrown against him and that he was likely to be trapped in Detroit. There was a general plan of campaign, submitted by Major General Henry Dearborn before the war began, which provided for a threefold invasion — from Sackett's Harbor on

Lake Ontario, from Niagara, and from Detroit —
in support of a grand attack along the route leading
past l   Champlain to Montreal.   Theoretically,
i*   d enough strategy, but no attempt had
          .de to prepare the execution, and there was
          ader competent to direct it.

In response to Hull's urgent appeal, Dearborn,
who was puttering about between Boston and Albany, confessed that he knew nothing about what
was going on at Niagara.   He ranked as the commander-in-chief of the American forces and he
awoke from his habitual stupor to ask himself this
amazing question: "Who is to have the command
of the operations in Upper Canada?   I take it for
granted that my command does not extend to that
distant quarter."   If Dearborn did not know who
was in control of the operations at Niagara, it was
safe to say that nobody else did, and Hull was left
to deal with the increasing forces in front of him
and the hordes of Indians in the rear, to garrison
Detroit, to assault the fort at Amherstburg, to
overcome the British naval forces on Lake Erie —
and all without the slightest help or coöperation
from his Government.

Meanwhile Brock had ascertained that the
American force at Niagara consisted of a few

hundred militia with no responsible officer in command, who were making a pretense of patrolling
thirty-six miles of frontier. They were undisci-
plined, ragged, without tents, shoes, money, or
munitions, and ready to fall back if attacked or
to go home unless soon relieved. Having nothing
to fear in that quarter, Brock gathered up a small
body of regulars as he marched and proceeded to
Amherstburg to finish the business of the unfortunate Hull.

That Hull deserves some pity as well as the disgrace which overwhelmed him is quite apparent.
Most of his troops were ill-equipped, unreliable, and
insubordinate. Even during the march to Detroit
he had to use a regular regiment to compel the obedience of twelve hundred mutinous militiamen who
refused to advance. Their own officer could do
nothing with them. At Detroit two hundred of
them refused to cross the river, on the ground that
they were not obliged to serve outside the United
States. Granted such extenuation as this, however, Hull showed himself so weak and contemptible in the face of danger that he could not expect
his fighting men to maintain any respect for him.

His fatal flaw was lack of courage and prompti-
tude. He did not know how to play a poor hand

well. In the emergency which confronted him he was like a dull sword in a rusty scabbard.   While the enemy waited for reinforcements, he might have captured Amherstburg. He had the superior force, and yet he delayed and lost heart while his regiments dwindled because of sickness and desertion and jeered at his leadership. The watchful Indians, led by the renowned Tecumseh, learned to despise the Americans instead of fearing them, and were eager to take the warpath against so easy a prey. Already other bands of braves were hastening from Lake Huron and from Mackinac, whose American garrison had been wiped out.

Brooding and shaken, like an old man utterly undone, Hull abandoned his pretentious invasion of Canada and retreated across the river to shelter his troops behind the log barricades of Detroit. He sent six hundred men to try to open a line to Ohio, but, after a sharp encounter with a British force, Hull was obliged to admit that they "could only open communication as far as the points of their bayonets extended." His only thought was to extricate himself, not to stand and fight a winning battle without counting the cost.   His officers felt only contempt for his cowardice.   They were convinced that the tide could be turned in their favor.

There were steadfast men in the ranks who were eager to take the measure of the redcoats. The colonels were in open mutiny and, determined to set General Hull aside, they offered the command to Colonel Miller of the regulars, who declined to accept it. When Hull proposed a general retreat, he was informed that every man of the Ohio militia would refuse to obey the order. These troops who had been so fickle and jealous of their rights were unwilling to share the leader's disgrace.

Two days after his arrival at Amherstburg, General Brock sent to the Americans a summons to surrender, adding with a crafty discernment of the effect of the threat upon the mind of the man with whom he was dealing: "You must be aware that the numerous body of Indians who have attached themselves to my troops will be beyond my control the moment the contest commences." Hull could see only the horrid picture of a massacre of the women and children within the stockades of Detroit. He failed to realize that his thousand effective infantrymen could hold out for weeks behind those log ramparts against Brock's few hundred regulars and volunteers. Two and a half years later, Andrew Jackson and his militia emblazoned a very different story behind the cypress

2

breastworks of New Orleans. Besides the thousand men in the fort, Hull had detached five hundred under Colonels McArthur and Cass to attempt to break through the Indian cordon in his
rear and obtain supplies. These he now vainly
endeavored to recall while he delayed a final reply
to Brock's mandate.

Indecision had doomed the garrison which was
now besieged. Tecumseh's warriors had crossed
the river and were between the fort and McArthur's
column. Brock boldly decided to assault, a desperate venture, but he must have known that Hull's
will had crumbled. No more than seven hundred
strong, the little British force crossed the river just
before daybreak on the 16th of August and was
permitted to select its positions without the slightest molestation. A few small field pieces, posted
on the Canadian side of the river, hurled shot into
the fort, killing four of Hull's men, and two British
armed schooners lay within range.

Brock advanced, expecting to suffer large losses
from the heavy guns which were posted to cover the
main approach to the fort, but his men passed
through the zone of danger and found cover in
which they made ready to storm the defenses of
Detroit. As Brock himself walked forward to take

note of the situation before giving the final commands, a white flag fluttered from the battery in front of him. Without firing a shot, Hull had surrendered Detroit and with it the great territory of Michigan, the most grievous loss of domain that the United States has ever suffered in war or peace. On the same day Fort Dearborn (Chicago), which had been forgotten by the Government, was burned by Indians after all its defenders had been slain. These two disasters with the earlier fall of Mackinac practically erased American dominion from the western empire of the Great Lakes. Visions of the conquest of Canada were thus rudely dimmed in the opening actions of the war.

General Hull was tried by court-martial on charges of treason, cowardice, and neglect of duty. He was convicted on the last two charges and sentenced to be shot, with a recommendation to the mercy of the President. The verdict was approved by Madison, but he remitted the execution of the sentence because of the old man's services in the Revolution. Guilty though he was, an angry and humiliated people also made him the scapegoat for the sins of neglect and omission of which their Government stood convicted. In the testimony offered at his trial there was a touch, rude, vivid, and very human, to portray him in the final hours of the tragic episode at Detroit.   Spurned by his officers, he sat on the ground with his back against the rampart while "he apparently unconsciously filled his mouth with tobacco, putting in quid after quid more than he generally did; the spittle colored with tobacco juice ran from his mouth on his neckcloth, beard, cravat, and vest."

Later events in the Northwest Territory showed that the British successes in that region were gained chiefly because of an unworthy alliance with the Indian tribes, whose barbarous methods of warfare stained the records of those who employed them.   "Not more than seven or eight hundred British soldiers ever crossed the Detroit River," says Henry Adams, "but the United States raised fully twenty thousand men and spent at least five million dollars and many lives in expelling them. The Indians alone made this outlay necessary. The campaign of Tippecanoe, the surrender of Detroit and Mackinaw, the massacres at Fort Dearborn, the river Raisin, and Fort Meigs, the murders along the frontier, and the campaign of 1813 were the prices paid for the Indian lands in the Wabash Valley."

Before the story shifts to the other fields of the

war, it seems logical to follow to its finally successful result the bloody, wasteful struggle for the re-
covery of the lost territory. This operation required large armies and long campaigns, together
with the naval supremacy of Lake Erie, won in the
next year by Oliver Hazard Perry, before the fugi-
tive British forces fell back from the charred ruins
of Detroit and Amherstburg and were soundly
beaten at the battle of the Thames — the one decisive, clean-cut American victory of the war on the
Canadian frontier. These events showed that far
too much had been expected of General William
Hull, who comprehended his difficulties but made
no attempt to batter a way through them, forget-
ting that to die and win is always better than to
live and fail.

CHAPTER II

LOST GROUND REGAINED

GENERAL WILLIAM HENRY HARRISON, the hero of
Tippecanoe and the Governor of Indiana Territory, whose capital was at Vincennes on the Wabash, possessed the experience and the instincts
of a soldier. He had foreseen that Hull, unless he received support, must either abandon
Detroit or be hopelessly hemmed in. The task
of defending the western border was ardently undertaken by the States of Kentucky and Ohio.
They believed in the war and were ready to aid it
with the men and resources of a vigorous population of almost a million. When the word came
that Hull was in desperate straits, Harrison hastened to organize a relief expedition. Before he
could move, Detroit had fallen. But a high tide
of enthusiasm swept him on toward an attempt
to recover the lost empire. The Federal Government approved his plans and commissioned him

as commander of the Northwestern army of ten thousand men.

In the early autumn of 1812, General Harrison launched his ambitious and imposing campaign, by which three separate bodies of troops were to advance and converge within striking distance of Detroit, while a fourth was to invade and destroy the nests of Indians on the Wabash and Illinois rivers. An active British force might have attacked and defeated these isolated columns one by one, for they were beyond supporting distance of each other; but Brock now needed his regulars for the defense of the Niagara frontier. The scattered American army, including brigades from Virginia and Pennsylvania, was too strong to be checked by Indian forays, but it had not reckoned with the obstacles of an unfriendly wilderness and climate. In October, no more than a month after the bugles had sounded the advance, the campaign was halted, demoralized and darkly uncertain. A vast swamp stretched as a barrier across the route and heavy rains made it impassable.

Hull had crossed the same swamp with his small force in the favorable summer season, but Harrison was unable to transport the food and war material needed by his ten thousand men. A million rations were required at the goal of the Maumee Rapids, and yet after two months of heartbreaking endeavor not a pound of provisions had been carried within fifty miles of this place. Wagons and pack-trains floundered in the mud and were abandoned. The rivers froze and thwarted the use of flotillas of scows. Winter closed down, and the American army was forlornly mired and blockaded along two hundred miles of front. The troops at Fort Defiance ate roots and bark. Typhus broke out among them, and they died like flies. For the failure to supply the army, the War Department was largely responsible, and Secretary Eustis very properly resigned in December. This removed one glaring incompetent from the list but it failed to improve Harrison's situation.

It was not until the severe frosts of January, 1813, fettered the swamps that Harrison was able to extricate his troops and forward supplies to the shore of Lake Erie for an offensive against Amherstburg. First in motion was the left wing of thirteen hundred Kentucky militia and regulars under General Winchester. This officer was an elderly planter who, like Hull, had worn a uniform in the Revolution. He had no great aptitude for war and was held in low esteem by the Kentuckians of his command — hungry, mutinous, and disgusted men, who were counting the days before their enlistments should expire. The commonplace Winchester was no leader to hold them in hand and spur their jaded determination.

While they were building storehouses and log defenses, within dangerously easy distance of the British post at Amherstburg, the tempting message came that the settlement of Frenchtown, on the Raisin, thirty miles away and within the British lines, was held by only two companies of Canadian militia. Here was an opportunity for a dashing adventure, and Winchester ordered half his total force to march and destroy this detachment of the enemy. The troops accordingly set out, drove home a brisk assault, cleared Frenchtown of its defenders, and held their ground awaiting orders.

Winchester then realized that he had leaped before he looked. He had seriously weakened his own force while the column at Frenchtown was in peril from two thousand hostile troops and Indians only eighteen miles beyond the river Raisin. The Kentuckians left with him decided matters for themselves. They insisted on marching to the support of their comrades at Frenchtown. Meanwhile General Harrison had learned of this fatuous

division of strength and was hastening to the base
at the falls of the Maumee.   There he found only
three hundred men.   All the others had gone with
Winchester to reinforce the men at Frenchtown.
It was too late to summon troops from other points,
and Harrison waited with forebodings of disaster.

News reached him after two days.   The Americans at the Raisin had suffered not only a defeat
but a massacre.   Nearly four hundred were killed
in battle or in flight.   Those who survived were
prisoners.   No more than thirty had escaped of a
force one thousand strong.   The enemy had won
this extraordinary success with five hundred white
troops and about the same number of Indians, led
by Colonel Procter, whom Brock had placed in
command of the fort at Amherstburg.   Procter's
name is infamous in the annals of the war.   The
worst traditions of Indian atrocity, uncontrolled
and even encouraged, cluster about his memory.
He was later promoted in rank instead of being de-
graded, a costly blunder which England came to
regret and at last redeemed.   A notoriously incompetent officer, on this one occasion of the battle
of the Raisin he acted with decision and took
advantage of the American blunder.

The conduct of General Winchester after his

arrival at Frenchtown is inexplicable. He did nothing to prepare his force for action even on learning that the British were advancing from Amherstburg. A report of the disaster, after recording that no patrols or pickets were ordered out during the night, goes on:

The troops were permitted to select, each for himself, such quarters on the west side of the river as might please him best, whilst the general took his quarters on the east side — not the least regard being paid to defense, order, regularity, or system in the posting of the different corps. . . . Destitute of artillery, or engineers, of men who had ever heard or seen the least of an enemy; and with but a very inadequate supply of ammunition — how he ever could have entertained the most distant hope of success, or what right he had to presume to claim it, is to me one of the strangest things in the world.

At dawn, on the 21st of January, the British and Indians, having crossed the frozen Detroit River the day before, formed within musket shot of the American lines and opened the attack with a battery of three-pounders. They might have rushed the camp with bayonet and tomahawk and killed most of the defenders asleep, but the cannonade alarmed the Kentuckians and they took cover behind a picket fence, using their long rifles so expertly that they killed or wounded a hundred and eighty-five of the British regulars, who thereupon had to abandon their artillery. Meanwhile, the American regular force, caught on open ground, was flanked and driven toward the river, carrying a militia regiment with it. Panic spread among these unfortunate men and they fled through the deep snow, Winchester among them, while six hundred whooping Indians slew and scalped them without mercy as they ran.

But behind the picket fence the Kentuckians still squinted along the barrels of their rifles and hammered home more bullets and patches. Three hundred and eighty-four of them, they showed a spirit that made their conduct the bright, heroic episode of that black day. Forgotten are their mutinies, their profane disregard of the Articles of War, their jeers at generals and such. They finished in style and covered the multitude of their sins. Unclothed, unfed, uncared for, dirty, and wretched, they proved themselves worthy to be called American soldiers. They fought until there was no more ammunition, until they were surrounded by a thousand of the enemy, and then they honorably surrendered.

The brutal Procter, aware that the Indians would

commit hideous outrages if left unrestrained, nevertheless returned to Amherstburg with his troops and his prisoners, leaving the American wounded to their fate. That night the savages came back to Frenchtown and massacred those hurt and helpless men, thirty in number.

This unhappy incident of the campaign, not so much a battle as a catastrophe, delayed Harrison's operations. His failures had shaken popular confidence, and at the end of this dismal winter, after six months of disappointments in which ten thousand men had accomplished nothing, he was compelled to report to the Secretary of War:

Amongst the reasons which make it necessary to employ a large force, I am sorry to mention the dismay and disinclination to the service which appears to prevail in the western country; numbers must give that confidence which ought to be produced by conscious valor and intrepidity, which never existed in any army in a superior degree than amongst the greater part of the militia which were with me through the winter. The new drafts from this State [Ohio] are entirely of another character and are not to be depended upon. I have no doubt, however, that a sufficient number of good men can be procured, and should they be allowed to serve on horseback, Kentucky would furnish some regiments that would not be inferior to those that fought at the river Raisin; and these were, in my opinion, superior to any militia that ever took the field in modern times.

There was to be no immediate renewal of action between Procter and Harrison. Each seemed to have conceived so much respect for the forces of the other that they proceeded to increase the distance between them as rapidly as possible. Fearing to be overtaken and greatly outnumbered, the British leader retreated to Canada while the American leader was in a state of mind no less uneasy. Harrison promptly set fire to his storehouses and supplies at the Maumee Rapids, his advanced base near Lake Erie. Thus all this labor and exertion and expense vanished in smoke while, in the set diction of war, he retired some fifteen miles. In such a vast hurry were the adversaries to be quit of each other that a day and a half after the fight at Frenchtown they were sixty miles apart. Harrison remained a fortnight on this back trail and collected two thousand of his troops, with whom he returned to the ruins of his foremost post and undertook the task all over again.

The defensive works which he now built were called Fort Meigs. For the time there was no more talk of invading Canada. The service of the

Kentucky and Ohio militia was expiring, and these seasoned regiments were melting away like snow. Presently Fort Meigs was left with no more than five hundred war-worn men to hold out against British operations afloat and ashore. Luckily Procter had expended his energies at Frenchtown and seemed inclined to repose, for he made no effort to attack the few weak garrisons which guarded the American territory near at hand. From January until April he neglected his opportunities while more American militia marched homeward, while Harrison was absent, while Fort Meigs was unfinished.

At length the British offensive was organized, and a thousand white soldiers and as many Indians, led by Tecumseh, sallied out of Amherstburg with a naval force of two gunboats. Heavy guns were dragged from Detroit to batter down the log walls, for it was the intention to surround and besiege Fort Meigs in the manner taught by the military science of Europe. Meanwhile Harrison had come back from a recruiting mission; and a new brigade of Kentucky militia, twelve hundred strong, under Brigadier General Green Clay, was to follow in boats down the Auglaize and Maumee rivers. Procter's guns were already pounding the walls of

Fort Meigs on the 5th of May when eight hundred troops of this fresh American force arrived within striking distance. They dashed upon the British batteries and took them with the bayonet in a wild, impetuous charge. It was then their business promptly to reform and protect themselves, but through lack of training they failed to obey orders and were off hunting the enemy, every man for himself. In the meantime three companies of British regulars and some volunteers took advantage of the confusion, summoned the Indians, and let loose a vicious counter-attack.

Within sight of General Harrison and the garrison of Fort Meigs, these bold Kentuckians were presently driven from the captured guns, scattered, and shot down or taken prisoner. Only a hundred and seventy of them got away, and they lost even their boats and supplies. The British loss was no more than fifty in killed and wounded. Again Procter inflamed the hatred and contempt of his American foes because forty of his prisoners were tomahawked while guarded by British soldiers. He made no effort to save them and it was the intervention of Tecumseh, the Indian leader, which averted the massacre of the whole body of five hundred prisoners.

Across the river, Colonel John Miller, of the American regular infantry, had attempted a gallant sortie from the fort and had taken a battery but this sally had no great effect on the issue of the engagement. Harrison had lost almost a thousand men, half his fighting force, and was again shut up within the barricades and blockhouses of Fort Meigs. Procter continued the siege only four days longer, for his Indian allies then grew tired of it and faded into the forest. He was not reluctant to accept this excuse for withdrawing. His own militia were drifting away, his regulars were suffering from illness and exposure, and Fort Meigs itself was a harder nut to crack than he had anticipated. Procter therefore withdrew to Amherstburg and made no more trouble until June, when he sent raiding parties into Ohio and created panic among the isolated settlements.

Harrison had become convinced that his campaign must be a defensive one only, until a strong American naval force could be mustered on Lake Erie. He moved his headquarters to Upper Sandusky and Cleveland and concluded to mark time while Perry's fleet was building. The outlook was somber, however, for his thin line of garrisons and his supply bases. They were threatened in all directions, but he was most concerned for the important depot which he had established at Upper Sandusky, no more than thirty miles from any British landing force which should decide to cross Lake Erie. The place had no fortifications; it was held by a few hundred green recruits; and the only obstacle to a hostile ascent of the Sandusky River was a little stockade near its mouth, called Fort Stephenson.

For the Americans to lose the accumulation of stores and munitions which was almost the only result of a year's campaign would have been a fatal blow. Harrison was greatly disturbed to hear that Tecumseh had gathered his warriors and was following the trail that led to Upper Sandusky and that Procter was moving coastwise with his troops in a flotilla under oars and sail. Harrison was, or believed himself to be, in grave danger of confronting a plight similar to that of William Hull, beset in front, in flank, in rear. His first thought was to evacuate the stockade of Fort Stephenson and to concentrate his force, although this would leave the Sandusky River open for a British advance from the shore of Lake Erie.

An order was sent to young Major Croghan, who held Fort Stephenson with one hundred and sixty men, to burn the buildings and retreat as fast as possible up the river or along the shore of Lake Erie. This officer, a Kentuckian not yet twenty-one years old, who honored the regiment to which he belonged, deliberately disobeyed his commander. By so doing he sounded a ringing note which was like the call of trumpets amidst the failures, the cloudy uncertainties, the lack of virile leadership, that had strewn the path of the war. In writing he sent this reply back to General William Henry Harrison: "We have determined to maintain this place, and by Heaven, we will."

It was a turning point, in a way, presaging more hopeful events, a warning that youth must be served and that the doddering oldsters were to give place to those who could stand up under the stern and exacting tests of warfare. Such rash ardor was not according to precedent. Harrison promptly relieved the impetuous Croghan of his command and sent a colonel to replace him. But Croghan argued the point so eloquently that the stockade was restored to him next day and he won his chance to do or die. Harrison consolingly informed him that he was to retreat if attacked by British troops "but that to attempt to retire in the face of an Indian force would be vain."

Major Croghan blithely prepared to do anything else than retreat, while General Harrison stayed ten miles away to plan a battle against Tecumseh's Indians if they should happen to come in his direction. On the 1st of August, Croghan's scouts informed him that the woods swarmed with Indians and that British boats were pushing up the river. Procter was on the scene again, and no sooner had his four hundred regulars found a landing place than a curt demand for surrender came to Major Croghan. The British howitzers peppered the stockade as soon as the refusal was delivered, but they failed to shake the spirit of the dauntless hundred and sixty American defenders. On the following day, the 2d of August, Procter stupidly repeated his error of a direct assault upon sheltered riflemen, which had cost him heavily at the Raisin and at Fort Meigs. He ordered his redcoats to carry Fort Stephenson. Again and again they marched forward until all the officers had been shot down and a fifth of the force was dead or wounded. American valor and marksmanship had proved themselves in the face of heavy odds. At sunset the beaten British were flocking into their boats, and Procter was again on his way to Amherstburg. His excuse for the trouncing laid the blame on the Indians:

The troops, after the artillery had been used for some hours, attacked two faces and, impossibilities being attempted, failed. The fort, from which the severest fire I ever saw was maintained during the attack, was well defended. The troops displayed the greatest bravery, the much greater part of whom reached the fort and made every effort to enter; but the Indians who had proposed the assault and, had it not been assented to, would have ever stigmatized the British character, scarcely came into fire before they ran out of its reach. A more than adequate sacrifice having been made to Indian opinion, I drew off the brave assailants.

The sound of Croghan's guns was heard in General Harrison's camp at Seneca, ten miles up the river. Harrison had nothing to say but this: "The blood be upon his own head. I wash my hands of it." This was a misguided speech which the country received with marked disfavor while it acclaimed young Croghan as the sterling hero of the western campaign. He could be also a loyal as well as a successful subordinate, for he ably defended Harrison against the indignation which menaced his station as commander of the army. The new Secretary of War, John Armstrong, ironically referred to Procter and Harrison as being always in terror of each other, the one actually flying from his supposed pursuer after his fiasco at

Fort Stephenson, the other waiting only for the arrival of Croghan at Seneca to begin a camp conflagration and flight to Upper Sandusky.

The reconquest of Michigan and the Northwest depended now on the American navy. Harrison wisely halted his inglorious operations by land until the ships and sailors were ready to coöperate. Because the British sway on the Great Lakes was unchallenged, the general situation of the enemy was immensely better than it had been at the beginning of the campaign. During a year of war the United States had steadily lost in men, in territory, in prestige, and this in spite of the fact that the opposing forces across the Canadian border were much smaller.

That the men of the American navy would be prompt to maintain the traditions of the service was indicated in a small way by an incident of the previous year on Lake Erie. In September, 1812, Lieutenant Jesse D. Elliott had been sent to Buffalo to find a site for building naval vessels. A few weeks later he was fitting out several purchased schooners behind Squaw Island. Suddenly there came sailing in from Amherstburg and anchored off Fort Erie two British armed brigs, the *Detroit* which had been surrendered by Hull, and the

Caledonia which had helped to subdue the American garrison at Mackinac. Elliott had no ships ready for action, but he was not to be daunted by such an obstacle. It so happened that ninety Yankee seamen had been sent across country from New York by Captain Isaac Chauncey. These worthy tars had trudged the distance on foot, a matter of five hundred miles, with their canvas bags on their backs, and they rolled into port at noon, in the nick of time to serve Elliott's purpose. They were indubitably tired, but he gave them not a moment for rest. A ration of meat and bread and a stiff tot of grog, and they turned to and manned the boats which were to cut out the two British brigs when darkness fell.

Elliott scraped together fifty soldiers and, filling two cutters with his amphibious company, he stole out of Buffalo and pulled toward Fort Erie. At one o'clock in the morning of the 9th of October they were alongside the pair of enemy brigs and together the bluejackets and the infantry tumbled over the bulwarks with cutlass, pistols, and boarding pike. In ten minutes both vessels were captured and under sail for the American shore. The *Caledonia* was safely beached at Black Rock, where Elliott was building his little navy yard. The wind, however, was so light that the *Detroit* was swept downward by the river current and had to anchor under the fire of British batteries. These she fought with her guns until all her powder was shot away. Then she cut her cable, hoisted sail again, and took the bottom on Squaw Island, where both British and American guns had the range of her. Elliott had to abandon her and set fire to the hull, but he afterward recovered her ordnance.

What Elliott had in mind shows the temper of this ready naval officer. "A strong inducement," he wrote, "was that with these two vessels and those I have purchased, I should be able to meet the remainder of the British force on the Upper Lakes." The loss of the *Detroit* somewhat disappointed this ambitious scheme but the success of the audacious adventure foreshadowed later and larger exploits with far-reaching results. Isaac Brock, the British general in Canada, had the genius to comprehend the meaning of this naval exploit. "This event is particularly unfortunate," he wrote, "and may reduce us to incalculable distress. The enemy is making every exertion to gain a naval superiority on both lakes; which, if they accomplish, I do not see how we can retain the country." And to Procter, his commander at

Detroit, he disclosed the meaning of the naval loss as it affected the fortunes of the western campaign: "This will reduce us to great distress. You will have the goodness to state the expedients you possess to enable us to replace, as far as possible, the heavy loss we have suffered in the *Detroit*."

But another year was required to teach the American Government the lesson that a few small vessels roughly pegged together of planks sawn from the forest, with a few hundred seamen and guns, might be far more decisive than the random operations of fifty thousand troops. This lesson, however, was at last learnt; and so, in the summer of 1813, General William Henry Harrison waited at Seneca on the Sandusky River until he received, on the 10th of September, the deathless despatch of Commodore Oliver Hazard Perry: "We have met the enemy and they are ours." The navy had at last cleared the way for the army.

Expeditiously forty-five hundred infantry were embarked and set ashore only three miles from the coveted fort at Amherstburg. A mounted regiment of a thousand Kentuckians, raised for frontier defense by Richard M. Johnson, moved along the road to Detroit. Harrison was about to square accounts with Procter, who had no stomach for a stubborn defense. Tecumseh, still loyal to the British cause, summoned thirty-five hundred of his warriors to the royal standard to stem this American invasion. They expected that Procter would offer a courageous resistance, for he had also almost a thousand hard-bitted British troops, seasoned by a year's fighting. But Procter's sun had set and disgrace was about to overtake him. To Tecumseh, a chieftain who had waged war because of the wrongs suffered by his own people, the thought of flight in this crisis was cowardly and intolerable. When Procter announced that he proposed to seek refuge in retreat, Tecumseh told him to his face that he was like a fat dog which had carried its tail erect and now that it was frightened dropped its tail between its legs and ran. The English might scamper as far as they liked but the Indians would remain to meet the American invaders.

It was a helter-skelter exodus from Amherstburg and Detroit. All property that could not be moved was burned or destroyed, and Procter set out for Moraviantown, on the Thames River, seventy miles along the road to Lake Ontario. Harrison, amazed at this behavior, reported: "Nothing but infatuation could have governed General Proctor's conduct. The day I landed below Malden [Amherstburg] he had at his disposal upward of three thousand Indian warriors; his regular force reinforced by the militia of the district would have made his number nearly equal to my aggregate, which on the day of landing did not exceed forty-five hundred. . . . His inferior officers say that his conduct has been a series of continued blunders."

Procter had put a week behind him before Harrison set out from Amherstburg in pursuit, but the British column was hampered in flight by the women and children of the deserted posts, the sick and wounded, the wagon trains, the stores, and baggage. The organization had gone to pieces because of the demoralizing example set by its leader. A hundred miles of wilderness lay between the fugitives and a place of refuge. Overtaken on the Thames River, they were given no choice. It was fight or surrender. Ahead of the American infantry brigades moved Johnson's mounted Kentuckians, armed with muskets, rifles, knives, and tomahawks, and led by a resourceful and enterprising soldier. Procter was compelled to form his lines of battle across the road on the north bank of the Thames or permit this formidable American cavalry to trample his straggling ranks under hoof.

Tecumseh's Indians, stationed in a swamp, covered his right flank and the river covered his left. Harrison came upon the enemy early in the afternoon of the 5th of October and formed his line of battle. The action was carried on in a manner "not sanctioned by anything that I had seen or heard of," said Harrison afterwards. This first American victory of the war on land was, indeed, quite irregular and unconventional. It was won by Johnson's mounted riflemen, who divided and charged both the redcoats in front and the Indians in the swamp. One detachment galloped through the first and second lines of the British infantry while the other drove the Indians into the American left wing and smashed them utterly. Tecumseh was among the slain. It was all over in one hour and twenty minutes. Harrison's foot soldiers had no chance to close with the enemy. The Americans lost only fifteen killed and thirty wounded, and they took about five hundred prisoners and all Procter's artillery, muskets, baggage, and stores.

Not only was the Northwest Territory thus regained for the United States but the power of the Indian alliance was broken. Most of the hostile tribes now abandoned the British cause. Tecumseh's confederacy of Indian nations fell to pieces

OLIVER HAZARD PERRY AT THE BATTLE OF LAKE ERIE

Painting by J. W. Jarvis. In the City Hall, New York, owned by the Corporation. Reproduced by courtesy of the Municipal Art Commission of the City of New York.

ISAAC CHAUNCEY

Painting in the Comptroller's Office, City Hall, New York, owned by the Corporation. Reproduced by courtesy of the Municipal Art Commission of the City of New York.

OLIVER HAZARD PERRY AT THE BATTLE OF LAKE
ERIE

Painting by J. W. Jarvis. In the City Hall, New York, owned by the Corporation. Reproduced by courtesy of the Municipal Art Commission of the City of New York.

ISAAC CHAUNCEY

Painting in the Comptroller's Office, City Hall, New York, owned by the Corporation. Reproduced by courtesy of the Municipal Art Commission of the City of New York.

with the death of its leader. The British army of Upper Canada, shattered and unable to receive reinforcements from overseas, no longer menaced Michigan and the western front of the American line. General Harrison returned to Detroit at his leisure, and the volunteers and militia marched homeward, for no more than two regular brigades were needed to protect all this vast area. The struggle for its possession was a closed episode. In this quarter, however, the war cry "On to Canada!" was no longer heard. The United States was satisfied to recover what it had lost with Hull's surrender and to rid itself of the peril of invasion and the horrors of Indian massacres along its wilderness frontiers. Of the men prominent in the struggle, Procter suffered official disgrace at the hands of his own Government and William Henry Harrison became a President of the United States.

CHAPTER III

AMID the prolonged vicissitudes of these western campaigns, two subordinate officers, the boyish Major Croghan at Fort Stephenson and the dashing Colonel Johnson with his Kentucky mounted infantry, displayed qualities which accord with the best traditions of American arms. Of kindred spirit and far more illustrious was Captain Oliver Hazard Perry of the United States Navy. Perry dealt with and overcame, on a much larger scale, similar obstacles and discouragements — untrained men, lack of material, faulty support — but was ready and eager to meet the enemy in the hour of need. If it is a sound axiom never to despise the enemy, it is nevertheless true that excessive prudence has lost many an action. Farragut's motto has been the keynote of the success of all the great sea-captains, *"L'audace, et encore de l'audace, et toujours de l'audace."*

46

It was not until the lesson of Hull's surrender had aroused the civil authorities that Captain Chauncey of the navy yard at New York received orders in September, 1812, "to assume command of the naval force on Lakes Erie and Ontario and to use every exertion to obtain control of them this fall." Chauncey was an experienced officer, forty years old, who had not rusted from inactivity like the elderly generals who had been given command of armies. He knew what he needed and how to get it. Having to begin with almost nothing, he busied himself to such excellent purpose that he was able to report within three weeks that he had forwarded to Sackett's Harbor on Lake Ontario, "one hundred and forty ship carpenters, seven hundred seamen and marines, more than one hundred pieces of cannon, the greater part of large caliber, with musket, shot, carriages, etc. The carriages have nearly all been made and the shot cast in that time. Nay, I may say that nearly every article that has been forwarded has been made."

It was found impossible to divert part of this ordnance to Buffalo because of the excessively bad roads, which were passable for heavy traffic only by means of sleds during the snows of winter. This obstacle spoiled the hope of putting a fighting force afloat on Lake Erie during the latter part of 1812. Chauncey consequently established his main base at Sackett's Harbor and lost no time in building and buying vessels. In forty-five days from laying the keel he launched a ship of the corvette class, a third larger than the ocean cruisers *Wasp* and *Hornet*, "and nine weeks ago," said he, "the timber that she is composed of was growing in the forest."

Lieutenant Elliott at the same time had not been idle in his little navy yard at Black Rock near Buffalo, where he had assembled a small brig and several schooners. In December Chauncey inspected the work and decided to shift it to Presqu' Isle, now the city of Erie, which was much less exposed to interference by the enemy. Here he got together the material for two brigs of three hundred tons each, which were to be the main strength of Perry's squadron nine months later. Impatient to return to Lake Ontario, where a fleet in being was even more urgently needed, Chauncey was glad to receive from Commander Oliver Hazard Perry an application to serve under him. To Perry was promptly turned over the burden and the responsibility of smashing the British naval power on Lake Erie. Events were soon to display the notable differences in temperament and capabilities between these two men. Though he had greater opportunities on Lake Ontario, Chauncey was too cautious and held the enemy in too much respect; wherefore he dodged and parried and fought inconclusive engagements with the fleet of Sir James Yeo until destiny had passed him by. He lives in history as a competent and enterprising chief of dockyards and supplies but not as a victorious seaman.

To Perry, in the flush of his youth at twenty-eight years, was granted the immortal spark of greatness to do and dare and the personality which impelled men gladly to serve him and to die for him. His difficulties were huge, but he attacked them with a confidence which nothing could dismay. First he had to concentrate his divided force. Lieutenant Elliott's flotilla of schooners at that time lay at Black Rock. It was necessary to move them to Erie at great risk of capture by the enemy, but vigilance and seamanship accomplished this feat. It then remained to finish and equip the larger vessels which were being built. Two of these were the brigs ordered laid down by Chauncey, the *Lawrence* and the *Niagara*. Apart from these, the battle squadron consisted of seven small schooners and the captured British brig, the

Caledonia. In size and armament they were absurd cockleshells even when compared with a modern destroyer, but they were to make themselves superbly memorable. Perry's flagship was no larger than the ancient coasting schooners which ply today between Bangor and Boston with cargoes of lumber and coal.

Through the winter and spring of 1813, the carpenters, calkers, and smiths were fitting the new vessels together from the green timber and planking which the choppers and sawyers wrought out of the forest. The iron, the canvas, and all the other material had to be hauled by horses and oxen from places several hundred miles distant. Late in July the squadron was ready for active service but was dangerously short of men. This, however, was the least of Perry's concerns. He had reckoned that seven hundred and forty officers and sailors were required to handle and fight his ships, but he did not hesitate to put to sea with a total force of four hundred and ninety.

Of these a hundred were soldiers sent him only nine days before he sailed, and most of them trod a deck for the first time. Chauncey was so absorbed in his own affairs and hazards on Lake Ontario that he was not likely to give Perry any more men than could be spared. This reluctance caused Perry to send a spirited protest in which he said: "The men that came by Mr. Champlin are a motley set, blacks, soldiers, and boys. I cannot think you saw them after they were selected."

As the superior officer, Chauncey resented the criticism and replied with this warning reproof: "As you have assured the Secretary that you should conceive yourself equal or superior to the enemy, with a force of men so much less than I had deemed necessary, there will be a great deal expected from you by your country, and I trust they will not be disappointed in the high expectations formed of your gallantry and judgment."

The quick temper of Perry flared at this. He was about to sail in search of the British fleet with what men he had because he was unable to obtain more, and he had rightly looked to Chauncey to supply the deficiency. Impulsively he asked to be relieved of his command and gave expression to his sense of grievance in a letter to the Secretary of the Navy in which he said, among other things: "I cannot serve under an officer who has been so totally regardless of my feelings. . . . The critical state of General Harrison was such that I took upon myself the responsibility of going out with the few

young officers you had been pleased to send me,
with the few seamen I had, and as many volunteers as I could muster from the militia.   I did not
shrink from this responsibility but, Sir, at that
very moment I surely did not anticipate the receipt
of a letter in every line of which is an insult."
Most fortunately Perry's request for transfer could
not be granted until after the battle of Lake Erie
had been fought and won.   The Secretary answered in tones of mild rebuke: "A change of
commander under existing circumstances, is equally
inadmissible as it respects the interest of the service and your own reputation.   It is right that you
should reap the harvest which you have sown."

Perry's indignation seems excusable.   He had
shown a cheerful willingness to shoulder the whole
load and his anxieties had been greater than his
superiors appeared to realize.   Captain Barclay,
who commanded the British naval force on Lake
Erie and who had been hovering off Erie while the
American ships were waiting for men, might readily
have sent his boats in at night and destroyed the
entire squadron.   Perry had not enough sailors to
defend his ships, and the regiment of Pennsylvania militia stationed at Erie to guard the naval
base refused to do duty on shipboard after dark

"I told the boys to go, Captain Perry," explained their worthless colonel, "but the boys won't go."

Perry's lucky star saved him from disaster, however, and on the 2d of August he undertook the perilous and awkward labor of floating his larger vessels over the shallow bar of the harbor at Erie. Barclay's blockading force had vanished. For Perry it was then or never. At any moment the enemy's topsails might reappear, and the American ships would be caught in a situation wholly defenseless. Perry first disposed his light-draft schooners to cover his channel, and then hoisted out the guns of the *Lawrence* brig and lowered them into boats. Scows, or "camels," as they were called, were lashed alongside the vessel to lift her when the water was pumped out of them. There was no more than four feet of water on the bar, and the brig-of-war bumped and stranded repeatedly even when lightened and assisted in every possible manner. After a night and a day of unflagging exertion she was hauled across into deep water and the guns were quickly slung aboard. The *Niagara* was coaxed out of harbor in the same ingenious fashion, and on the 4th of August Perry was able to report that all his vessels were over the bar, although Barclay had returned by now and "the enemy had been in sight all day."

Perry endeavored to force an engagement without delay, but the British fleet retired to Amherstburg because Barclay was waiting for a new and powerful ship, the *Detroit,* and he preferred to spar for time. The American vessels thereupon anchored off Erie and took on stores. They had fewer than three hundred men aboard, and it was bracing news for Perry to receive word that a hundred officers and men under Commander Jesse D. Elliott were hastening to join him. Elliott became second in command to Perry and assumed charge of the *Niagara.*

For almost a month the Stars and Stripes flew unchallenged from the masts of the American ships. Perry made his base at Put-in Bay, thirty miles southeast of Amherstburg, where he could intercept the enemy passing eastward. The British commander, Barclay, had also been troubled by lack of seamen and was inclined to postpone action. He was nevertheless urged on by Sir George Prevost, the Governor General of Canada, who told him that "he had only to dare and he would be successful." A more urgent call on Barclay to fight was due to the lack of food in the Amherstburg region, where the water route was now blockaded by the American ships. The British were feeding fourteen thousand Indians, including warriors and their families, and if provisions failed the red men would be likely to vanish.

At sunrise of the 10th of September, a sailor at the masthead of the *Lawrence* sighted the British squadron steering across the lake with a fair wind and ready to give battle. Perry instantly sent his crews to quarters and trimmed sail to quit the bay and form his line in open water. He was eager to take the initiative, and it may be assumed that he had forgotten Chauncey's prudent admonition: "The first object will be to destroy or cripple the enemy's fleet; but in all attempts upon the fleet you ought to use great caution, for the loss of a single vessel may decide the fate of a campaign."

Small, crude, and hastily manned as were the ships engaged in this famous fresh-water battle, it should be borne in mind that the proven principles of naval strategy and tactics used were as sound and true as when Nelson and Rodney had demonstrated them in mighty fleet actions at sea. In the final council in his cabin, Perry echoed Nelson's words in saying that no captain could go very far wrong who placed his vessel close alongside those of the enemy.   Chauncey's counsel, on the other hand, would have lost the battle.   Perry's decision to give and take punishment, no matter if it should cost him a ship or two, won him the victory.

The British force was inferior, both in the number of vessels and the weight of broadsides, but this inferiority was somewhat balanced by the greater range and hitting power of Barclay's longer guns. Each had what might be called two heavy ships of the line: the British, the *Detroit* and the *Queen Charlotte*, and the Americans, the *Lawrence* and the *Niagara*.   Next in importance and fairly well matched were the *Lady Prevost* under Barclay's flag and the *Caledonia* under Perry's.   There remained the light schooner craft of which the American squadron had six and the British only three. Perry realized that if he could put ship against ship the odds would be largely in his favor, for, with his batteries of carronades which threw their shot but a short distance, he would be unwise to maneuver for position and let the enemy pound him to pieces at long range.   His plan of battle was therefore governed entirely by his knowledge of Barclay's strength and of the possibilities of his own forces.

With a light breeze and working to windward,

Perry's ship moved to intercept the British squadron which lay in column, topsails aback and waiting. The American brigs were fanned ahead by the air which breathed in their lofty canvas, but the schooners were almost becalmed and four of them straggled in the rear, their crews tugging at the long sweeps or oars. Two of the faster of these, the *Scorpion* and the *Ariel*, were slipping along in the van where they supported the American flagship *Lawrence*, and Perry had no intention of delaying for the others to come up. Shortly before noon Barclay opened the engagement with the long guns of the *Detroit*, but as yet Perry was unable to reach his opponent and made more sail on the *Lawrence* in order to get close.

The British gunners of the *Detroit* were already finding the target, and Perry discovered that the *Lawrence* was difficult to handle with much of her rigging shot away. He ranged ahead until his ship was no more than two hundred and fifty yards from the *Detroit*. Even then the distance was greater than desirable for the main battery of carronades. A good golfer can drive his tee shot as far as the space of water which separated these two indomitable flagships as they fought. It was a different kind of naval warfare from that of today in which superdreadnaughts score hits at battle ranges of twelve and fourteen miles.

Perry's plans were now endangered by the failure of his other heavy ship, the *Niagara*, to take care of her own adversary, the *Queen Charlotte*, which forged ahead and took a station where her broadsides helped to reduce the *Lawrence* to a mass of wreckage.   A bitter dispute which challenged the courage and judgment of Commander Elliott of the *Niagara* was the aftermath of this flaw in the conduct of the battle.   It was charged that he failed to go to the support of his commander-in-chief when the flagship was being destroyed under his eyes.   The facts admit of no doubt: he dropped astern and for two hours remained scarcely more than a spectator of a desperate action in which his ship was sorely needed, whereas if he had followed the order to close up, the *Lawrence* need never have struck to the enemy.

In his defense he stated that lack of wind had prevented him from drawing ahead to engage and divert the *Queen Charlotte* and that he had been instructed to hold a certain position in line.   At the time Perry found no fault with him, merely setting down in his report that "at half-past two, the wind springing up, Captain Elliott was enabled to bring

his vessel, the *Niagara*, gallantly into close action."
Later Perry formulated charges against his second
in command, accusing him of having kept on a
course "which would in a few minutes have carried
said vessel entirely out of action." These documents were pigeonholed and a Court of Inquiry
commended Elliott as a brave and skillful officer
who had gained laurels in that "splendid victory."

The issue was threshed out by naval experts
who violently disagreed, but there was glory enough
for all and the flag had suffered no stain.   Certain
it is that the battle would have lacked its most
brilliantly dramatic episode if Perry had not been
compelled to shift his pennant from the blazing
hulk of the *Lawrence* and, from the quarter-deck of
the *Niagara*, to renew the conflict, rally his vessels,
and snatch a triumph from the shadow of disaster.
It was one of the great moments in the storied
annals of the American navy, comparable with a
John Paul Jones shouting "*We have not yet begun to
fight!*" from the deck of the shattered, water-logged
Bon Homme Richard, or a Farragut lashed in the
rigging and roaring "*Damn the torpedoes!   Full
speed ahead!*"

Because of the failure of Elliott to bring the
Niagara into action at once, as had been laid down

in the plan of battle, Perry found himself in desperate straits aboard the beaten *Lawrence*. Her colors still flew but she could fire only one gun of her whole battery, and more than half the ship's company had been killed or wounded — eighty-three men out of one hundred and forty-two. It was impossible to steer or handle her and she drifted helpless. Then it was that Perry, seeing the laggard *Niagara* close at hand, ordered a boat away and was transferred to a ship which was still fit and ready to continue the action. As soon as he had left them, the survivors of the *Lawrence* hauled down their flag in token of surrender, for there was nothing else for them to do.

As soon as he jumped on deck, Perry took command of the *Niagara*, sending Elliott off to bring up the rearmost schooners. There was no lagging or hesitation now. With topgallant sails sheeted home, the *Niagara* bore down upon the *Detroit*, driven by a freshening breeze. Barclay's crippled flagship tried to avoid being raked and so fouled her consort, the *Queen Charlotte*. The two British ships lay locked together while the American guns pounded them with terrific fire. Presently they got clear of each other and pluckily attempted to carry on the fight. But the odds were hopeless.

The officer whose painful duty it was to signal the surrender of the *Detroit* said of this British flagship: "The ship lying completely unmanageable, every brace cut away, the mizzen-topmast and gaff down, all the other masts badly wounded, not a stay left forward, hull shattered very much, a number of guns disabled, and the enemy's squadron raking both ships ahead and astern, none of our own in a position to support us, I was under the painful necessity of answering the enemy to say we had struck, the *Queen Charlotte* having previously done so."

It was later reported of the *Detroit* that it was "impossible to place a hand upon that broadside which had been exposed to the enemy's fire without covering some portion of a wound, either from grape, round, canister, or chain shot." The crew had suffered as severely as the vessel. The valiant commander of the squadron, Captain Barclay, was a fighting sailor who had lost an arm at Trafalgar. In the battle of Lake Erie he was twice wounded and had to be carried below. His first lieutenant was mortally hurt and in the critical moments the ship was left in charge of the second lieutenant. In this gallant manner did Perry and Barclay, both heirs of the bulldog Anglo-Saxon strain, wage their bloody duel without faltering and thus did the British sailor keep his honor bright in defeat.

The little American schooners played a part in smashing the enemy. The *Ariel* and *Scorpion* held their positions in the van and their long guns helped deal the finishing blows to the *Detroit*, while the others came up when the breeze grew stronger and engaged their several opponents. The *Caledonia* was effective in putting the *Queen Charlotte* out of action. When the larger British ships surrendered, the smaller craft were compelled to follow the example, and the squadron yielded to Perry after three hours of battle. It was in no boastful strain but as the laconic fact that he sent his famous message to the nation. He had met the enemy and they were all his. It was leadership — brilliant and tenacious — which had employed makeshift vessels, odd lots of guns, and crews which included militia, sick men, and "a motley set of blacks and boys." Barclay had labored under handicaps no less heavy, but it was his destiny to match himself against a superior force and a man of unquestioned naval genius. Oliver Hazard Perry would have made a name for himself, no doubt, if his career had led him to blue water and the command of stately frigates.

On Lake Ontario, Chauncey dragged his naval campaign through two seasons and then left the enemy in control. Perry, by opening the way for Harrison, rewon the Northwest for the United States because he sagaciously upheld the doctrine of Napoleon that "war cannot be waged without running risks." Behind his daring, however, lay tireless, painstaking preparation and a thorough knowledge of his trade.

CHAPTER IV

THE events of the war by land are apt to be as confusing in narration as they were in fact. The many forays, skirmishes, and retreats along the Canadian frontier were campaigns in name only, ambitiously conceived but most haltingly executed. Major General Dearborn, senior officer of the American army, had failed to begin operations in the center and on the eastern flank in time to divert the enemy from Detroit; but in the autumn of 1812 he was ready to attempt an invasion of Canada by way of Niagara. The direct command was given to Major General Stephen Van Rensselaer of the New York State militia, who was to advance as soon as six thousand troops were assembled. At first Dearborn seemed hopeful of success. He predicted that "with the militia and other troops there or on the march, they will be able, I presume, to cross over into Canada, carry

64

all the works in Niagara, and proceed to the other posts in that province in triumph."

The fair prospect soon clouded, however, and Dearborn, who was of a doubtful, easily discouraged temperament, partly due to age and infirmities, discovered that "a strange fatality seemed to have pervaded the whole arrangements." Yet this was when the movement of troops and supplies was far brisker and better organized than could have been expected and when the armed strength was thrice that of Brock, the British general, who was guarding forty miles of front along the Niagara River with less than two thousand men. At Queenston which was the objective of the first American attack there were no more than two companies of British regulars and a few militia, in all about three hundred troops. The rest of Brock's forces were at Chippawa and Fort Erie, where the heavy assaults were expected.

An American regular brigade was on the march to Buffalo, but its commander, Brigadier General Alexander Smyth, was not subordinate to Van Rensselaer, and the two had quarreled. Smyth paid no attention to a request for a council of war and went his own way. On the night of the 10th of October Van Rensselaer attempted to cross the

5

Niagara River, but there was some blunder about the boats and the disgruntled troops returned to camp. Two nights later they made another attempt but found the British on the alert and failed to dislodge them from the heights of Queenston. A small body of American regulars, led by gallant young Captain Wool, managed to clamber up a path hitherto regarded as impassable. There they held a precarious position and waited for help. Brock, who was commanding the British in person, was instantly killed while storming this hillside at the head of reinforcements. In him the enemy lost its ablest and most intrepid leader.

The forenoon wore on and Captain Wool, painfully wounded, still clung to the heights with his two hundred and fifty men. A relief column which crossed the river found itself helpless for lack of artillery and intrenching tools and was compelled to fall back. Van Rensselaer forgot his bickering with General Smyth and sent him urgent word to hasten to the rescue. Winfield Scott, then a lieutenant colonel, came forward as a volunteer and took command of young Captain Wool's forlorn hope. Gradually more men trickled up the heights until the ground was defended by three hundred and fifty regulars and two hundred and fifty militia.

Meanwhile the British troops were mustering up the river at Chippawa, and the red lines of their veterans were descried advancing from Fort George below. Bands of Indians raced by field and forest to screen the British movements and to harass the American lines. The tragic turn of events appears to have dazed General Van Rensselaer. The failure to save the beleaguered and outnumbered Americans on the heights he blamed upon his troops, reporting next day that his reinforcements embarked very slowly. "I passed immediately over to accelerate them," said he, "but to my utter astonishment I found that at the very moment when complete victory was in our hands the ardor of the unengaged troops had entirely subsided. I rode in all directions, urged the men by every consideration to pass over; but in vain."

The candid fact seems to be that this general of militia had made a sorry mess of the whole affair, and his men had lost all faith in his ability to turn the adverse tide. He stood and watched six hundred valiant American soldiers make their last stand on the rocky eminence while the British hurled more and more men up the slope. One concerted attack by the idle American army would have swept them away like chaff. But there was only

one Winfield Scott in the field, and his lot was cast
with those who fought to the bitter end as a sacrifice to stupidity. The six hundred were surrounded. They were pushed back by weight of opposing numbers. Still they died in their tracks,
until the survivors were actually pushed over a
cliff and down to the bank of the river.

There they surrendered, for there were no boats
to carry them across. The boatmen had fled to
cover as soon as the Indians opened fire on them.
Winfield Scott was among the prisoners together
with a brigadier general and two more lieutenant
colonels who had been bagged earlier in the day.
Ninety Americans were killed and many more
wounded, while a total of nine hundred were captured during the entire action. Van Rensselaer
had lost almost as many troops as Hull had lost at
Detroit, and he had nothing to show for it. He
very sensibly resigned his command on the next day.

The choice of his successor, however, was again
unfortunate. Brigadier General Alexander Smyth
had been inspector general in the regular army
before he was given charge of an infantry brigade.
He had a most flattering opinion of himself, and
promotion to the command of an army quite turned
his head. The oratory with which he proceeded

and there he abandoned his personal conquest of Canada. His army literally melted away, "about four thousand men without order or restraint discharging their muskets in every direction," writes an eyewitness. They riddled the general's tent with bullets by way of expressing their opinion of him, and he left the camp not more than two leaps ahead of his earnest troops. He requested permission to visit his family, after the newspapers had branded him as a coward, and the visit became permanent. His name was dropped from the army rolls without the formality of an inquiry. It seemed rather too much for the country to ~~bear~~ that, in the first year of the war, its armies ~~should~~ have suffered from the failures of Hull, Van ~~Rensselaer~~, and Smyth.

~~It~~ had been hoped that General Dearborn might ~~carry~~ out his own idea of an operation against ~~Montreal~~ at the same time as the Niagara campaign ~~was~~ in progress. On the shore of Lake Champlain Dearborn was in command of the largest and ~~most~~ promising force under the American flag, including seven regiments of the regular army. Taking personal charge at Plattsburg, he marched this body of troops twenty miles in the direction of the Canadian border. Here the militia refused to go on, and he marched back again after four days in the field.   Beset with rheumatism and low spirits, he wrote to the Secretary of War: "I had anticipated disappointment and misfortune in the commencement of the war, but I did by no means apprehend such a deficiency of regular troops and such a series of disasters as we have witnessed." Coupled with this complaint was the request that he might be allowed "to retire to the shades of private life and remain a mere but interested spectator of passing events."

The Government, however, was not yet ready to release Major General Dearborn but instructed him to organize an offensive which should obta... control of the St. Lawrence River and thereby communication between Upper and Lower Can... This was the pet plan of Armstrong when h... came Secretary of War, and as soon as was po... he set the military machinery in motion.   In... ruary, 1813, Armstrong told Dearborn to ass... four thousand men at Sackett's Harbor, on... Ontario, and three thousand at Buffalo. ... larger force was to cross the lake in the spring, p... tected by Chauncey's fleet, capture the important naval station of Kingston, then attack York (Toronto), and finally join the corps at Buffalo for another operation against the British on the Niagara River. But Dearborn was not eager for the enterprise. He explained that he lacked sufficient strength for an operation against Kingston. With the support of Commodore Chauncey he proposed a different offensive which should be aimed first against York, then against Niagara, and finally against Kingston. This proposal reversed Armstrong's programme, and he permitted it to sway his decision. Thus the war turned westward from the St. Lawrence.

The only apparent success in this campaign occurred at York, the capital of Upper Canada, where on the 27th of April one ship under construction was burned and another captured after the small British garrison had been driven inland. The public buildings were also destroyed by fire, though Dearborn protested that this was done against his orders. In the next year, however, the enemy retaliated by burning the Capitol at Washington. The fighting at York was bloody, and the American forces counted a fifth killed or wounded. They remained on the Canadian side only ten days and then returned to disembark at Niagara. Here Dearborn fell ill, and his chief of staff, Colonel Winfield Scott, was left in virtual control of the army.

In May, 1813, most of the troops at Plattsburg
and Sackett's Harbor were moved to the Niagara
region for the purpose of a grand movement to take
Fort George, at the mouth of that river, from the
rear and thus redeem the failure of the preceding
campaign. Commodore Chauncey with his Ontario fleet was prepared to coöperate and to transport the troops. Three American brigadiers, Boyd,
Winder, and Chandler, effected a landing in hand-
some fashion, while Winfield Scott led an advance
division. Under cover of the ships they proceeded
along the beach and turned the right flank of the
British defenses. Fort George was evacuated, but
most of the force escaped and made their way
to Queenston, whence they continued to retreat
westward along the shore of Lake Ontario. Vincent, the British general, reported his losses in
killed and wounded and missing as three hundred
and fifty-six. The Americans suffered far less. It
was a clean-cut, workmanlike operation, and, according to an observer, "Winfield Scott fought
nine-tenths of the battle." But the chief aim
had been to destroy the British force, and in this
the adventure failed.

General Dearborn was not at all reconciled to
letting the garrison of Fort George get clean away

from him, and he therefore sent General Winder in pursuit with a thousand men. These were reinforced by as many more; and together they followed the trail of the retreating British to Stony Creek and camped there for the night. Vincent and his sixteen hundred British regulars were in bivouac ten miles beyond. The mishap at Fort George had by no means knocked the fight out of them. Vincent himself led six hundred men back in the middle of a black night (the 6th of June) and fell upon the American camp. A confused battle followed. The two forces intermingled in cursing, stabbing, swirling groups. The American generals, Chandler and Winder, walked straight into the enemy's arms and were captured. The British broke through and took the American batteries but failed to keep them. At length both parties retired, badly punished. The Americans had lost all ardor for pursuit and on the following day retreated ten miles and were soon ordered to return to Fort George.

General Dearborn was much distressed by this unlucky episode and was in such feeble health that he again begged to be relieved. He was, he said, "so reduced in strength as to be incapable of any command." General Morgan Lewis took temporary command at Niagara, but, being soon called to Sackett's Harbor, he was succeeded by General Boyd, whom Lewis was kind enough to describe, by way of recommendation, in these terms: "A compound of ignorance, vanity, and petulance, with nothing to recommend him but that species of bravery in the field which is vaporing, boisterous, stifling reflection, blinding observation, and better adapted to the bully than the soldier."

In order to live up to this encomium, Boyd sent Colonel Boerstler on the 24th of June, with four hundred infantry and two guns, to bombard and take an annoying stone house a day's march from Fort George. But two hundred hostile Indians so alarmed Boerstler that he attempted to retreat. Thirty hostile militia then caused him to halt the retreat and send for reinforcements. The reinforcements came to the number of a hundred and fifty, but the British also appeared with forty-seven more men. Colonel Boerstler thereupon surrendered his total of five hundred and forty soldiers. General Dearborn, still the nominal commander of the forces, sadly mentioned the disaster as "an unfortunate and unaccountable event."

There is a better account to be given, however, of events at Sackett's Harbor in this same month

of May. The operations on the Niagara front
had stripped this American naval base of troops
and of the protection of Chauncey's fleet. Sir
George Prevost, the Governor in Chief of Canada,
could not let the opportunity slip, although he was
not notable for energy. He embarked with a force
of regulars, eight hundred men, on Sir James Yeo's
ships at Kingston and sailed across Lake Ontario.

Sackett's Harbor was defended by only four hundred regulars of several regiments and about two
hundred and fifty militia from Albany. Couriers
rode through the countryside as soon as the British
ships were sighted, and several hundred volunteers
came straggling in from farm and shop and mill.
In them was something of the old spirit of Lexing-
ton and Bunker Hill, and to lead them there was
a real man and a soldier with his two feet under
him, Jacob Brown, a brigadier general of the state
militia, who consented to act in the emergency.
He knew what to do and how to communicate to
his men his own unshaken courage. On the beach
of the beautiful little harbor he posted five hundred
of his militia and volunteers to hamper the British
landing. His second line was composed of regulars. In rear were the forts with the guns manned.

The British grenadiers were thrown ashore at

dawn on the 28th of May under a wicked fire from American muskets and rifles, but their disciplined ranks surged forward, driving the militia back at the point of the bayonet and causing even the regulars to give ground.   The regulars halted at a blockhouse, where they had also the log barracks and timbers of the shipyard for a defense, and there they stayed in spite of the efforts of the British grenadiers to dislodge them.   Jacob Brown, stout-hearted and undismayed, rallied his militia in new positions.   Of the engagement a British officer said: "I do not exaggerate when I tell you that the shot, both of musketry and grape, was falling about us like hail. . . .   Those who were left of the troops behind the barracks made a dash out to charge the enemy; but the fire was so destructive that they were instantly turned by it, and the retreat was sounded.   Sir George, fearless of danger and disdaining to run or to suffer his men to run, repeatedly called out to them to retire in order; many, however, made off as fast as they could."

Before the retreat was sounded, the British expedition had suffered severely.   One man in three was killed or wounded, and the rest of them narrowly escaped capture.   Jacob Brown serenely reported to General Dearborn that "the militia were all rallied before the enemy gave way and were marching perfectly in his view towards the rear of his right flank; and I am confident that even then, if Sir George had not retired with the utmost precipitation to his boats, he would have been cut off."

Though he had given the enemy a sound thrashing, Jacob Brown found his righteous satisfaction spoiled by the destruction of the naval barracks, shipping, and storehouses. This was the act of a flighty lieutenant of the American navy who concluded too hastily that the battle was lost and therefore set fire to the buildings to keep the supplies and vessels out of the enemy's hands. Jacob Brown in his straightforward fashion emphatically placed the blame where it belonged:

The burning of the marine barracks was as infamous a transaction as ever occurred among military men. The fire was set as the enemy met our regulars upon the main line; and if anything could have appalled these gallant men it would have been the flames in their rear. We have all, I presume, suffered in the public estimation in consequence of this disgraceful burning. The fact is, however, that the army is entitled to much higher praise than though it had not occurred. The navy alone are responsible for what happened on Navy Point and it is fortunate for them that they have reputations sufficient to sustain the shock.

A few weeks later General Dearborn, after his repeated failures to shake the British grip on the Niagara front and the misfortunes which had darkened his campaigns, was retired according to his wish. But the American nation was not yet rid of its unsuccessful generals. James Wilkinson, who was inscrutably chosen to succeed Dearborn, was a man of bad reputation and low professional standing. "The selection of this unprincipled imbecile," said Winfield Scott, "was not the blunder of Secretary Armstrong." Added to this, Wilkinson was a man of broken health. He was shifted from command at New Orleans because the Southern Senators insisted that he was untrustworthy and incompetent. The regular army regarded him with contempt.

Secretary Armstrong endeavored to mend matters by making his own headquarters at Sackett's Harbor, where the next offensive, directed against Montreal, was planned under his direction. Success hung upon the coöperation and junction of two armies moving separately, the one under Wilkinson descending the St. Lawrence, the other under Wade Hampton setting out from Plattsburg on Lake Champlain. The fact that these two officers had hated each other for years made a difficult problem no easier. Hampton possessed uncommon ability and courage, but he was proud and sensitive, as might have been expected in a South Carolina gentleman, and he loathed Wilkinson with all his heart. That he should yield the seniority to one whom he considered a blackguard was to him intolerable, and he accepted the command on Lake Champlain with the understanding that he would take no orders from Wilkinson until the two armies were combined.

The expedition from Sackett's Harbor was ready to advance by way of the St. Lawrence in October, 1813, and comprised seven thousand effective troops. Even then the commanding general and the Secretary of War had begun to regard the adventure as dubious and were accusing each other of dodging the responsibility. Said Wilkinson to Armstrong: "It is necessary to my justification that you should, by the authority of the President, direct the operations of the army under my command particularly against Montreal." Said Armstrong to Wilkinson: "I speak conjecturally, but should we surmount every obstacle in descending the river we shall advance upon Montreal ignorant of the force arrayed against us and in case of misfortune having no retreat, the army must surrender

6

at discretion." This was scarcely the spirit to inspire a conquering army. As though to clinch his lack of faith in the enterprise, the Secretary of War ordered winter quarters built for ten thousand men many miles this side of Montreal, explaining in later years that he had suspected the campaign would terminate as it did, "with the disgrace of doing nothing."

On the 17th of October the army embarked in bateaux and coasted along Lake Ontario to the entrance of the St. Lawrence. After being delayed by stormy weather, the flotilla passed the British guns across from Ogdensburg and halted twenty miles below. There Wilkinson called a council of war to decide whether to proceed or retreat. Four generals voted to attack Montreal and two were reluctant but could see "no other alternative." Wilkinson then became ill and was unable to leave his boat or to give orders. Several British gunboats evaded Chauncey's blockade and annoyed the rear of the expedition. Eight hundred British infantry from Kingston followed along shore and peppered the boats with musketry and canister wherever the river narrowed. Finally it became necessary for the Americans to land a force to drive the enemy away. Jacob Brown took a brigade and cleared the bank in advance of the flotilla which floated down to a farm called Chrystler's and moored for the night.

General Boyd, who had been sent back with a strong force to protect the rear, reported next morning that the enemy was advancing in column. He was told to turn back and attack. This he did with three brigades. It was a brilliant opportunity to capture or destroy eight hundred British troops led by a dashing naval officer, Captain Mulcaster. Boyd lived up to his reputation, which was such that Jacob Brown had refused to serve under him. At this engagement of Chrystler's Farm, with two thousand regulars at his disposal, he was unmercifully beaten. Both Wilkinson and Morgan Lewis were flat on their backs, too feeble to concern themselves with battles. The American troops fought without a coherent plan and were defeated and broken in detail. Almost four hundred of them were killed, wounded, or captured. Their conduct reflected the half-hearted attitude of their commanding general and some of his subordinates. The badly mauled brigades hastily took to the boats and ran the rapids, stopping at the first harbor below. There Wilkinson received tidings from Wade Hampton's army which caused him to abandon the voyage down the St. Lawrence, and it is fair to conjecture that he shed no tears of disappointment.

In September Hampton had led his forces, recruited to four thousand infantry and a few dragoons, from Lake Champlain to the Canadian border in faithful compliance with his instructions to join the movement against Montreal. His line of march was westward to the Chateauguay River where he took a position which menaced both Montreal and that vital artery, the St. Lawrence. Building roads and bringing up supplies, he waited there for Wilkinson to set his own undertaking in motion. Word came from Secretary Armstrong to advance along the river, hold the enemy in check, and prepare to unite with Wilkinson's army. Hampton acted promptly and alarmed the British at Montreal, who foresaw grave consequences and assembled troops from every quarter. Hampton then learned that his army faced an enemy which was of vastly superior strength and which had every advantage of natural defense, while he himself was becoming convinced that Wilkinson was a broken reed and that no further support could be expected from the Government. General Prevost's own reports and letters showed that he had collected in the Montreal district and available for defense at least fifteen thousand rank and file, including the militia which had been mustered to repel Hampton's advance. The American position at Chateauguay was not less perilous than that of Harrison on the Maumee and far more so than that which had cost Dearborn so many disasters at Niagara.

Hampton moved forward half-heartedly. He had received a message from the War Department that his troops were to prepare winter quarters and these orders confirmed his suspicions that no attempt against Montreal was intended. "These papers sunk my hopes," he wrote in reply, "and raised serious doubts of that efficacious support that had been anticipated. I would have recalled the column, but it was in motion and the darkness of the night rendered it impracticable."

The last words refer to a collision with a small force of Canadian militia, led by Lieutenant Colonel de Salaberry, who had come forward to impede the American advance. These Canadians had obstructed the road with fallen trees and abatis, falling back until they found favorable ground where they very pluckily intrenched themselves. The intrepid party was comprised of a few Glengarry Fencibles and three hundred French-Canadian

Voltigeurs. Colonel de Salaberry was a trained soldier, and he now displayed brilliant courage and resourcefulness. Two American divisions attacking him were unable to carry his breastworks and were driven along the river bank and routed. Hampton's troops abandoned much of their equipment, and returned to camp with a loss of about fifty men.

There was great rejoicing in Canada and rightly so, for a victory had been handsomely won without the aid of British regulars; and Colonel de Salaberry's handful of French Canadians received the credit for thwarting the American plans against Montreal. But, without belittling the signal valor of the achievement, the documentary evidence goes to prove that Hampton's failure was largely due to the neglect of his Government. His state of mind at this time was such that he wrote: "Events have no tendency to change my opinion of the destiny intended for me, nor my determination to retire from a service where I can feel neither security nor expect honor."

With this tame conclusion the armies of Wilkinson and Hampton tucked themselves into log huts for the winter. Both accused the Secretary of War of leading them into an impossible venture and of then deserting them, while he in his turn accepted their resignations from the army. The fiasco was a costly one in quite another direction, for the Niagara sector had been overlooked in the elaborate attempt to capture Montreal. The few American troops who had gained a foothold on the Canadian side, at Fort George and the village of Niagara, were left unsupported while all the available regulars were sent to the armies of Wilkinson and Hampton. As soon as the British comprehended that the grand invasion had crumbled, they bethought themselves of the tempting opportunity to recover their forts at Niagara.

Wilkinson advised that the Americans evacuate Fort George, which they did on the 10th of December, when five hundred British soldiers were marching to retake it. There was no effort to reinforce the garrison, although at the time ten thousand American troops were idle in winter quarters. Fort Niagara, on the American side, still flew the Stars and Stripes, but on the night of the 18th of December Colonel Murray with five hundred and fifty British regulars rushed the fort, surprised the sentries, and lost only eight men in capturing this stronghold and its three hundred and fifty defenders. It was more like a massacre. Sixty-seven Americans were killed by the bayonet. A few nights later the Indian allies were loosed against Buffalo and Black Rock and ravaged thirty miles of frontier. The settlements were helpless. The Government had made not the slightest attempt to protect or defend them.

The war had come to the end of its second year, and by land the United States had done no more than to regain what Hull lost at Detroit. The conquest of Canada was a shattered illusion, a sorry tale of wasted energy, misdirected armies, sordid intrigue, lack of organization. A few worthless generals had been swept into the rubbish heap where they belonged, and this was the chief item on the credit side of the ledger. The state militia system had been found wanting; raw levies, defying authority and miserably cared for, had been squandered against a few thousand disciplined British regulars. The nation, angry and bewildered, was taking these lessons to heart. The story of 1814 was to contain far brighter episodes.

CHAPTER V

IT has pleased the American mind to regard the War of 1812 as a maritime conflict. This is natural enough, for the issue was the freedom of the sea, and the achievements of Yankee ships and sailors stood out in brilliant relief against the somber background of the inefficiency of the army. The offensive was thought to be properly a matter for the land forces, which had vastly superior advantages against Canada, while the navy was compelled to act on the defensive against overwhelming odds. The truth is that the navy did amazingly well, though it could not prevent the enemy's squadrons from blockading American ports or raiding the coasts at will. A few single ship actions could not vitally influence the course of the war; but they served to create an imperishable renown for the flag and the service, and to deal a staggering blow to the pride and prestige of an enemy whose ancient boast it was that Britannia ruled the waves.

The amazing thing is that the navy was able to accomplish anything at all, neglected and almost despised as it was by the same opinion which had suffered the army system to become a melancholy jest. During the decade in which Great Britain captured hundreds of American merchant ships in time of peace and impressed more than six thousand American seamen, the United States built two sloops-of-war of eighteen guns and allowed three of her dozen frigates to hasten to decay at their mooring buoys. Officers in the service were underpaid and shamefully treated by the Government. Captain Bainbridge, an officer of distinction, asked for leave that he might earn money to support himself, giving as a reason: "I have hitherto refused such offers on the presumption that my country would require my services. That presumption is removed, and even doubts entertained of the permanency of the naval establishment."

But, though Congress refused to build more frigates or to formulate a programme for guarding American shores and commerce, the tiny navy kept alive the spark of duty and readiness, while the nation drifted inevitably towards war. There was no scarcity of capable seamen, for the merchant marine was an admirable training-school. In those far-off days the technique of seafaring and sea fighting was comparatively simple. The merchant seaman could find his way about a frigate, for in rigging, handling, and navigation the ships were very much alike. And the American seamen of 1812 were in fighting mood; they had been whetted by provocation to a keen edge for war. They understood the meaning of "Free Trade and Sailors' Rights," if the landsmen did not. There were strapping sailors in every deep-water port to follow the fife and drum of the recruiting squad. The militia might quibble about "rights," but all the sailors asked was the weather gage of a British man-of-war. They had no patience with such spokesmen as Josiah Quincy, who said that Massachusetts would not go to war to contest the right of Great Britain to search American vessels for British seamen. They had neither forgotten nor forgiven the mortal affront of 1807, when their frigate *Chesapeake*, flying the broad pennant of Commodore James Barron, refused to let the British *Leopard* board and search her, and was fired into without warning and reduced to submission, after twenty-one of the American crew had been killed or wounded.

That shameful episode was in keeping with the attitude of the British navy toward the armed ships of the United States, "a few fir-built things with bits of striped bunting at their mast-heads," as George Canning, British Secretary of State for Foreign Affairs, described them. Long before the declaration of war British squadrons hovered off the port of New York to ransack merchant vessels or to seize them as prizes. In the course of the Napoleonic wars England had met and destroyed the navies of all her enemies in Europe. The battles of Copenhagen, the Nile, Trafalgar, and a hundred lesser fights had thundered to the world the existence of an unconquerable sea power.

Insignificant as it was, the American naval service boasted a history and a high morale. Its ships had been active. The younger officers served with seniors who had sailed and fought with Biddle and Barney and Paul Jones in the Revolution. Many of them had won promotions for gallantry in hand-to-hand combats in boarding parties, for following the bold Stephen Decatur in 1804 when he cut out and set fire to the *Philadelphia*, which had fallen into the hands of pirates at Tripoli, and helping Thomas Truxtun in 1799–1800 when the *Constellation* whipped the Frenchmen, *L'Insurgente*

COMMODORE STEPHEN DECATUR

and *La Vengeance*. In wardroom or steerage almost every man could tell of engagements in which he had behaved with credit. Trained in the school of hard knocks, the sailor knew the value of discipline and gunnery, of the smart ship and the willing crew, while on land the soldier rusted and lost his zeal.

The bluejackets were volunteers, not impressed men condemned to brutal servitude, and they had fought to save their skins in merchant vessels which made their voyages, in peril of privateer, pirate, and picaroon, from the Caribbean to the China Sea. The American merchant marine was at the zenith of its enterprise and daring, attracting the pick and flower of young manhood, and it offered incomparable material for the naval service and the fleets of swift privateers which swarmed out to harry England's commerce.[1]

The American frigates which humbled the haughty Mistress of the Seas beyond all precedent were superior in speed and hitting power to anything of their class afloat. It detracts not at all from the glory they won to remember that in every instance they were larger and of better design and

[1] For an account of the privateers of 1812, see *The Old Merchant Marine*, by Ralph D. Paine (in *The Chronicles of America*).

armament than the British frigates which they shot to pieces with such methodical accuracy.

When war was declared, the American Government was not quite clear as to what should be done with the navy. In New York harbor was a squadron of five ships under Commodore John Rodgers, including two of the heavier frigates or forty-fours, the *President* and the *United States*. Rodgers had also the lighter frigate *Congress*, the brig *Argus*, and the sloop *Hornet*. His orders were to look for British cruisers which were annoying commerce off Sandy Hook, chase them away, and then return to port for "further more extensive and particular orders." One hour after receiving these instructions the eager Rodgers put out to sea, with Captain Stephen Decatur as a squadron commander. The quarry was the frigate *Belvidera*, the most offensive of the British blockading force. This warship was sighted by the *President* and overtaken within forty-eight hours. An unlucky accident then occurred. Instead of running alongside, the *President* began firing at a distance and was hulling the enemy's stern when a gun on the forecastle burst and killed or wounded sixteen American sailors. Commodore Rodgers was picked up with a broken leg. Meanwhile the *Belvidera* cast overboard her boats and anchors, emptied the fresh water barrels to better her sailing trim, and, crowding on every stitch of canvas, drew away and was lost to view. Rodgers then forgot his orders to return to New York and went off in search of the great convoy of British merchant vessels homeward bound from Jamaica, which was called the plate fleet. He sailed as far as the English Channel before quitting the chase and then cruised back to Boston.

Meanwhile Captain Isaac Hull of the *Constitution* had taken on a crew and stores at Annapolis and was bound up the coast to New York. Hull's luck appeared to be no better than Rodgers's. Off Barnegat he sailed almost into a strong British squadron, which had been sent from Halifax. The escape from this grave predicament was an exploit of seamanship which is among the treasured memories of the service. It was the beginning of the career of the *Constitution*, whose name is still the most illustrious on the American naval list and whose commanders, Hull and Bainbridge, are numbered among the great captains. It is a privilege to behold today, in the Boston Navy Yard, this gallant frigate preserved as a heritage, her tall masts and graceful yards soaring above the grim, gray citadels that we call battleships. True it is that a single modern shell would destroy this obsolete, archaic frigate which once swept the seas like a meteor, but the very image of her is still potent to thrill the hearts and animate the courage of an American seaman.

On that luckless July morning, at break of day, off the New Jersey coast, it seemed as though the *Constitution* would be flying British colors ere she had a chance to fight. On her leeward side stood two English frigates, the *Guerrière* and the *Belvidera*, with the *Shannon* only five miles astern, and the rest of the hostile fleet lifting topsails above the southern horizon.

Not a breath of wind stirred. Captain Hull called away his boats, and the sailors tugged at the oars, towing the *Constitution* very slowly ahead. Captain Broke of the *Shannon* promptly followed suit and signaled for all the boats of the squadron. In a long column they trailed at the end of the hawser; and the *Shannon* crept closer. Catspaws of wind ruffled the water, and first one ship and then the other gained a few hundred yards as upper tiers of canvas caught the faint impulse. The *Shannon* was a crack ship, and there was no better crew in the British navy, as Lawrence of the *Chesapeake* afterwards learned to his mortal sorrow.

Gradually the *Shannon* cut down the intervening distance until she could make use of her bow guns.

At this Captain Hull resolved to try kedging his ship along, sending a boat half a mile ahead with a light anchor and all the spare rope on board. The crew walked the capstan round and hauled the ship up to the anchor, which they then lifted, carried ahead, and dropped again. The *Constitution* kept two kedges going all through that summer day, but the *Shannon* was playing the same game, and the two ships maintained their relative positions. They shot at each other at such long range that no damage was done. Before dusk the *Guerrière* caught a slant of breeze and worked nearer enough to bang away at the *Constitution*, which was, indeed, between the devil and the deep sea.

Night came on. The sailors, British and American, toiled until they dropped in their tracks, pulling at the kedge anchors and hawsers or bending to the sweeps of the cutters which towed at intervals and were exposed to the spatter of shot. It seemed impossible that the *Constitution* could slip clear of this pack of able frigates which trailed her like hounds. Toward midnight the fickle breeze awoke and wafted the ships along under studding sails and all the light cloths that were wont to

7

arch skyward. For two hours the men slept on
deck like logs while those on watch grunted at the
pump-brakes and the hose wetted the canvas to
make it draw better.

The breeze failed, however, and through the
rest of the night it was kedge and tow again, the
Shannon and the *Guerrière* hanging on doggedly,
confident of taking their quarry. Another day
dawned, hot and windless, and the situation was
unchanged. Other British ships had crawled or
drifted nearer, but the *Constitution* was always just
beyond range of their heavy guns. We may imag-
ine Isaac Hull striding across the poop and back
again, ruddy, solid, composed, wearing a cocked
hat and a gold-laced coat, lifting an eye aloft,
or squinting through his brass telescope, while he
damned the enemy in the hearty language of
the sea. He was a nephew of General William
Hull, but it would have been unfair to remind
him of it.

Near sunset of the second day of this unique test
of seamanship and endurance, a rain squall swept
toward the *Constitution* and obscured the ocean.
Just before the violent gust struck the ship her seamen scampered aloft and took in the upper sails.
This was all that safety required, but, seeing a

chance to trick the enemy, Hull ordered the lower sails double-reefed as though caught in a gale of wind. The British ships hastily imitated him before they should be overtaken in like manner and veered away from the chase. Veiled in the rain and dusk, the *Constitution* set all sail again and foamed at twelve knots on her course toward a port of refuge. Though two of the British frigates were in sight next morning, the *Constitution* left them far astern and reached Boston safely.

Seafaring New England was quick to recognize the merit of this escape. Even the Federalists, who opposed and hampered the war by land, were enthusiastic in praise of Captain Hull and his ship. They had outsailed and outwitted the best of the British men-of-war on the American coast, and a general feeling of hopelessness gave way to an ardent desire to try anew the ordeal of battle. With this spirit firing his officers and crew, Hull sailed again a few days later on a solitary cruise to the eastward with the intention of vexing the enemy's merchant trade and hopeful of finding a frigate willing to engage him in a duel. From Newfoundland he cruised south until a Salem privateer spoke him on the 18th of August and reported a British warship close by. The *Constitution* searched until the afternoon of the next day and then sighted her old friend, the *Guerrière*.

To retell the story of their fight in all the vanished sea lingo of that day would bewilder the landman and prove tedious to those familiar with the subject. The boatswains piped the call, "all hands clear ship for action"; the fife and drum beat to quarters; and four hundred men stood by the tackles of the muzzle-loading guns with their clumsy wooden carriages, or climbed into the tops to use their muskets or trim sail. Decks were sanded to prevent slipping when blood flowed. Boys ran about stacking the sacks of powder or distributing buckets of pistols ready for the boarding parties. And against the masts the cutlasses and pikes stood ready.

Captain John Dacres of the ill-fated *Guerrière* was an English gentleman as well as a gallant officer. But he did not know his antagonist. Like his comrades of the service he had failed to grasp the fact that the *Constitution* and the other American frigates of her class were the most formidable craft afloat, barring ships of the line, and that they were to revolutionize the design of war-vessels for half a century thereafter. They were frigates, or cruisers, in that they carried guns on two decks, but the main battery of long twenty-four-pound guns was an innovation, and the timbers and planking were stouter than had ever been built into ships of the kind. So stout, indeed, were the sides that shot rebounded from them more than once and thus gave the *Constitution* the affectionate nickname of "Old Ironsides."

Sublimely indifferent to these odds, Captain Dacres had already sent a challenge, with his compliments, to Commodore Rodgers of the United States frigate *President*, saying that he would be very happy to meet him or any other American frigate of equal force, off Sandy Hook, "for the purpose of having a few minutes' tête-à-tête." It was therefore with the utmost willingness that the *Constitution* and the *Guerrière* hoisted their battle ensigns and approached each other warily for an hour while they played at long bowls, as was the custom, each hoping to disable the other's spars or rigging and so gain the advantage of movement. Finding this sort of action inconclusive, however, Hull set more sail and ran down to argue it with broadsides, coolly biding his time, although Morris, his lieutenant, came running up again and again to beg him to begin firing. Men were being killed beside their guns as they stood ready to jerk the lock strings.   The two ships were abreast of each other and no more than a few yards apart before the *Constitution* returned the cannonade that thundered from every gun port of her adversary.

Within ten minutes the *Guerrière's* mizzenmast was knocked over the side and her hull was shattered by the accurate fire of the Yankee gunners, who were trained to shoot on the downward roll of their ship and so smash below the water line.   Almost unhurt, the *Constitution* moved ahead and fearfully raked the enemy's deck before the ships fouled each other.   They drifted apart before the boarders could undertake their bloody business, and then the remaining masts of the British frigate toppled overside and she was a helpless wreck. Seventy-nine of her crew were dead or wounded and the ship was sinking beneath their feet.   Captain Isaac Hull could truthfully report: "In less than thirty minutes from the time we got alongside of the enemy she was left without a spar standing, and the hull cut to pieces in such a manner as to make it difficult to keep her above water."

Captain Dacres struck his flag, and the American sailors who went aboard found the guns dismounted, the dead and dying scattered amid a wild tangle of spars and rigging, and great holes blown through the sides and decks. The *Constitution* had suffered such trifling injury that she was fit and ready for action a few hours later. Of her crew only seven men were killed and the same number hurt. She was the larger ship, and the odds in her favor were as ten to seven, reckoned in men and guns, for which reasons Captain Hull ought to have won. The significance of his victory was that at every point he had excelled a British frigate and had literally blown her out of the water. His crew had been together only five weeks and could fairly be called green while the *Guerrière*, although short-handed, had a complement of veteran tars. The British navy had never hesitated to engage hostile men-of-war of superior force and had usually beaten them. Of two hundred fights between single ships, against French, Spanish, Italian, Russian, Danish, and Dutch, the English had lost only five. The belief of Captain Dacres that he could beat the *Constitution* was therefore neither rash nor ill-founded.

The English captain had ten Americans in his crew, but he would not compel them to fight against their countrymen and sent them below, although he sorely needed every man who could haul at a gun-tackle or lay out on a yard. Wounded though he was and heartbroken by the disaster, his chivalry was faultless, and he took pains to report: "I feel it my duty to state that the conduct of Captain Hull and his officers toward our men has been that of a brave and generous enemy, the greatest care being taken to prevent our men losing the smallest trifle and the greatest attention being paid to the wounded."

When the Englishman was climbing up the side of the *Constitution* as a prisoner, Isaac Hull ran to help him, exclaiming, "Give me your hand, Dacres. I know you are hurt." No wonder that these two captains became fast friends. It is because sea warfare abounds in such manly incidents as these that the modern naval code of Germany, as exemplified in the acts of her submarine commanders, was so peculiarly barbarous and repellent.

On board the *Guerrière* was Captain William B. Orne, of the Salem merchant brig *Betsy*, which had been taken as a prize. His story of the combat is not widely known and seems worth quoting in part:

At two P.M. we discovered a large sail to windward bearing about north from us. We soon made her out to be a frigate. She was steering off from the wind, with her head to the southwest, evidently with the intention of cutting us off as soon as possible. Signals were soon made by the *Guerrière*, but as they were not answered the conclusion was, of course, that she was either a French or American frigate. Captain Dacres appeared anxious to ascertain her character and after looking at her for that purpose, handed me his spyglass, requesting me to give him my opinion of the stranger. I soon saw from the peculiarity of her sails and from her general appearance that she was, without doubt, an American frigate, and communicated the same to Captain Dacres. He immediately replied that he thought she came down too boldly for an American, but soon after added, "The better he behaves, the more honor we shall gain by taking him."

When the strange frigate came down to within two or three miles' distance, he hauled upon the wind, took in all his light sails, reefed his topsails, and deliberately prepared for action. It was now about five o'clock in the afternoon when he filled away and ran down for the *Guerrière*. At this moment Captain Dacres politely said to me: "Captain Orne, as I suppose you do not wish to fight against your own countrymen, you are at liberty to go below the water-line." It was not long after this before I retired from the quarter-deck to the cock-pit; of course I saw no more of the action until the firing ceased, but I heard and felt much of its effects; for soon after I left the deck the firing commenced on board the *Guerrière*, and was kept up almost incessantly until about six o'clock when I heard a tremendous explosion from the opposing frigate. The effect of her shot seemed to make the *Guerrière* reel and tremble as though she had received the shock of an earthquake.

Immediately after this, I heard a tremendous crash

on deck and was told that the mizzen-mast was shot away. In a few moments afterward, the cock-pit was filled with wounded men. After the firing had ceased I went on deck and there beheld a scene which it would be difficult to describe: all the *Guerrière's* masts were shot away and, as she had no sails to steady her, she lay rolling like a log in the trough of the sea. Many of the men were employed in throwing the dead overboard. The decks had the appearance of a butcher's slaughter-house; the gun tackles were not made fast and several of the guns got loose and were surging from one side to the other.

Some of the petty officers and seamen, after the action, got liquor and were intoxicated; and what with the groans of the wounded, the noise and confusion of the enraged survivors of the ill-fated ship rendered the whole scene a perfect hell.

Setting the hulk of the *Guerrière* on fire, Captain Hull sailed for Boston with the captured crew. The tidings he bore were enough to amaze an American people which expected nothing of its navy, which allowed its merchant ships to rot at the wharves, and which regarded the operations of its armies with the gloomiest forebodings. New England went wild with joy over a victory so peculiarly its own. Captain Hull and his officers were paraded up State Street to a banquet at Faneuil Hall while cheering thousands lined the sidewalks. A few days earlier had come the news of the surrender of Detroit, but the gloom was now dispelled. Americans could fight, after all. Popular toasts of the day were:

OUR INFANT NAVY—*We must nurture the young Hercules in his cradle, if we mean to profit by the labors of his manhood.*

THE VICTORY WE CELEBRATE—*An invaluable proof that we are able to defend our rights on the ocean.*

Handbills spread the news through the country, and artillery salutes proclaimed it from Carolina to the Wabash. Congress voted fifty thousand dollars as prize money to the heroes of the *Constitution* and medals to her officers. The people of New York gave them swords, and Captain Hull and Lieutenant Morris received pieces of plate from the patriots of Philadelphia. Federalists laid aside for the moment their opposition to the war and proclaimed that their party had founded and supported the navy. The moral effect of the victory was out of all proportion to its strategic importance. It was like sunshine breaking through a fog. Such rejoicing had been unknown, even in the decisive moments of the War of the Revolution. It served to show how deep-seated had been the American conviction that Britain's mastery of the sea was like a spell which could not be broken.

CHAPTER VI

MATCHLESS FRIGATES AND THEIR DUELS

IT was soon made clear that the impressive victory over the *Guerrière* was neither a lucky accident nor the result of prowess peculiar to the *Constitution* and her crew. Ship for ship, the American navy was better than the British. This is a truth which was demonstrated with sensational emphasis by one engagement after another. During the first eight months of the war there were five such duels, and in every instance the enemy was compelled to strike his colors. In tavern and banquet hall revelers were still drinking the health of Captain Isaac Hull when the thrilling word came that the *Wasp*, an eighteen-gun ship or sloop, as the type was called in naval parlance, had beaten the *Frolic* in a rare fight. The antagonists were so evenly matched in every respect that there was no room for excuses, and on both sides were displayed such stubborn hardihood and a seamanship so dauntless

"CONSTITUTION" AND "GUERRIÈRE"

An old print, illustrating the moment in the action at which the mainmast of the *Guerrière*, shattered by the terrific fire of the American frigate, fell overside, transforming the former vessel into a floating wreck and terminating the action. The picture represents accurately the surprisingly slight damage done the *Constitution;* note the broken spanker gaff and the shot holes in her topsails.

as to make an Anglo-Saxon proud that these foemen were bred of a common stock.

The *Wasp* had sailed from the Delaware on the 13th of October, heading southeast to look for British merchantmen in the West India track. Her commander was Captain Jacob Jones, a name revived in modern days by a destroyer of the Queenstown fleet in the arduous warfare against the German submarines. Shattered by a torpedo, the *Jacob Jones* sank in seven minutes, and sixty-four of the officers and crew perished, doing their duty to the last, disciplined, unafraid, so proving themselves worthy of the American naval service and of the memory of the unflinching captain of 1812.

The little *Wasp* ran into a terrific gale which blew her sails away and washed men overboard. But she made repairs and stood bravely after a British convoy which was escorted by the eighteen-gun brig *Frolic*, Captain Thomas Whinyates. The *Frolic*, too, had been battered by the weather, and the cargo ships had been scattered far and wide. The *Wasp* sighted several of them in the moonlight but, fearing they might be war vessels, followed warily until morning revealed on her leeward side the *Frolic*. Jacob Jones promptly shortened sail, which was the nautical method of rolling up one's sleeves, and steered close to attack.

It seemed preposterous to try to fight while the seas were still monstrously swollen and their crests were breaking across the decks of these vessels of less than five hundred tons burden. Wildly they rolled and pitched, burying their bows in the roaring combers. The merchant ships which watched this audacious defiance of wind and wave were having all they could do to avoid being swept or dismasted. Side by side wallowed *Wasp* and *Frolic*, sixty yards between them, while the cannon rolled their muzzles under water and the gunners were blinded with spray. Britisher and Yank, each crew could hear the hearty cheers of the other as they watched the chance to ply rammer and sponge and fire when the deck lifted clear of the sea.

Somehow the *Wasp* managed to shoot straight and fast. They were of the true webfooted breed in this hard-driven sloop-of-war, but there were no fair-weather mariners aboard the *Frolic*, and they hit the target much too often for comfort. Within ten minutes they had saved Captain Jacob Jones the trouble of handling sail, for they shot away his upper masts and yards and most of his rigging. The *Wasp* was a wreck aloft but the *Frolic* had suffered more vitally, for as usual the American gun captains aimed for the deck and hull; and they had been carefully drilled at target practice. The British sailors suffered frightfully from this storm of grape and chain shot, but those who were left alive still fought inflexibly. It looked as though the *Frolic* might get away, for the masts of the *Wasp* were in danger of tumbling over the side. With this mischance in mind, Captain Jacob Jones shifted helm and closed in for a hand-to-hand finish.

For a few minutes the two ships plunged ahead so near each other that the rammers of the American sailors struck the side of the *Frolic* as they drove the shot down the throats of their guns. It was literally muzzle to muzzle. Then they crashed together and the *Wasp's* jib-boom was thrust between the *Frolic's* masts. In this position the British decks were raked by a murderous fire as Jacob Jones trumpeted the order, "Boarders away!" Jack Lang, a sailor from New Jersey, scrambled out on the bowsprit, cutlass in his fist, without waiting to see if his comrades were with him, and dropped to the forecastle of the *Frolic*. Lieutenant Biddle tried it by jumping on the bulwark and climbing to the other ship as they crashed together on the next heave of the sea, but a doughty midshipman, seeking a handy purchase, grabbed him by the coat tails and they fell back upon their own deck. Another attempt and Biddle joined Jack Lang by way of the bowsprit. These two thus captured the *Frolic*, for as they dashed aft the only living men on deck were the undaunted sailor at the wheel and three officers, including Captain Whinyates and Lieutenant Wintle, who were so severely wounded that they could not stand without support. They tottered forward and surrendered their swords, and Lieutenant Biddle then leaped into the rigging and hauled the British ensign down.

Of the *Frolic's* crew of one hundred and ten men only twenty were unhurt, and these had fled below to escape the dreadful fire from the *Wasp*. The gun deck was strewn with bodies, and the waves which broke over the ship swirled them to and fro, the dead and the wounded together. Not an officer had escaped death or injury. The *Wasp* was more or less of a tangle aloft but her hull was sound and only five of her men had been killed and five wounded. No sailors could have fought more bravely than Captain Whinyates and his British crew, but they had been overwhelmed in

three-quarters of an hour by greater skill, coolness,
and judgment.

No sea battle of the war was more brilliant than
this, but Captain Jacob Jones was delayed in sailing home to receive the plaudits due him. His
prize crew was aboard the *Frolic*, cleaning up the
horrid mess and fitting the beaten ship for the
voyage to Charleston, and the *Wasp* was standing
by when there loomed in sight a towering three-
decker — a British ship of the line — the *Poictiers*.
The *Wasp* shook out her sails to make a run for
it, but they had been cut to ribbons and she was
soon overhauled. Now an eighteen-gun ship could
not argue with a majestic seventy-four. Captain
Jacob Jones submitted with as much grace as he
could muster, and *Wasp* and *Frolic* were carried
to Bermuda. The American crew was soon ex-
changed, and Congress applied balm to the injured
feelings of these fine sailormen by filling their
pockets to the amount of twenty-five thousand
dollars in prize money.

It was only a week later that the navy vouchsafed an encore to a delighted nation. This time
the sport royal was played between stately frigates.
On the 8th of October Commodore Rodgers had
taken his squadron out of Boston for a second

8

cruise. After four days at sea the *United States* was detached, and Captain Stephen Decatur ranged off to the eastward in quest of diversion. A fortnight of monotony was ended by a strange sail which proved to be the British thirty-eight-gun frigate *Macedonian,* newly built. Her commander, Captain Carden, had the highest opinion of his ship and crew, and one of his officers testified that "the state of discipline on board was excellent; in no British ship was more attention paid to gunnery. Before this cruise the ship had been engaged almost every day with the enemy; and in time of peace the crew were constantly exercised at the great guns."

The *United States* was a sister frigate of the *Constitution,* built from the same designs and therefore more formidable than her British opponent as three is to two. Captain Carden had no misgivings, however, and instantly set out in chase of the American frigate. But he was unfortunate enough to pit himself against one of the ablest officers afloat, and his own talent was mediocre. The result was partly determined by this personal equation in an action in which the *Macedonian* was outgeneraled as well as outfought. And again gunnery was a decisive factor. Observers said that the broadsides of the *United States* flamed with such rapidity that the ship looked as though she were on fire.

Early in the fight Captain Carden bungled an opportunity to pass close ahead of the *United States* and so rake her with a destructive attack. Then rashly coming to close quarters, the *Macedonian* was swept by the heavy guns of the American frigate and reduced to wreckage in ninety minutes. The weather was favorable for the Yankee gun crews, and the war offered no more dramatic proof of their superbly intelligent training. The *Macedonian* had received more than one hundred shot in her hull, several below the water line, one mast had been cut in two, and the others were useless. More than a hundred of her officers and men were dead or injured. The *United States* was almost undamaged, a few ropes and small spars were shot away, and only twelve of her men were on the casualty list. Captain Decatur rightfully boasted that he had as fine a crew as ever walked a deck, American sailors who had been schooled for the task with the greatest care. English opinion went so far as to concede this much: "As a display of courage the character of our service was nobly upheld, but we would be deceiving ourselves were we to admit that the comparative expertness of the crews in gunnery was equally satisfactory. Now taking the difference of effect as given by Captain Carden, we must draw this conclusion — that the comparative loss in killed and wounded, together with the dreadful account he gives of the condition of his own ship, while he admits that the enemy's vessel was in comparatively good order, must have arisen from inferiority in gunnery as well as in force."

Decatur sent the *Macedonian* to Newport as a trophy of war and forwarded her battle flag to Washington. It arrived just when a great naval ball was in progress to celebrate the capture of the *Guerrière*, whose ensign was already displayed from the wall. It was a great moment for the young lieutenant of the *United States*, who had been assigned this duty, when he announced his mission and, amid the cheers of the President, the Cabinet, and other distinguished guests, proudly exhibited the flag of another British frigate to decorate the ballroom!

Meanwhile the *Constitution* had returned to sea to spread her royals to the South Atlantic trades and hunt for lumbering British East-Indiamen. Captain Isaac Hull had gracefully given up the command in favor of Captain William Bainbridge, who was one of the oldest and most respected officers of his rank and who deserved an opportunity to win distinction.   Bainbridge had behaved heroically at Tripoli and was logically in line to take over one of the crack frigates.   The sailors of the *Constitution* grumbled a bit at losing Isaac Hull but soon regained their alert and willing spirit as they comprehended that they had another first-rate "old man" in William Bainbridge.   Henry Adams has pointed out that the average age of Bainbridge, Hull, Rodgers, and Decatur was thirty-seven, while that of the four generals most conspicuous in the disappointments of the army, Dearborn, Wilkinson, William Hull, and Wade Hampton, was fifty-eight. The difference is notable and is mentioned for what it may be worth.

Through the autumn of 1812 the frigate cruised beneath tropic suns, much of the time off the coast of Brazil.   Today the health and comfort of the bluejacket are so scrupulously provided for in every possible way that a battleship is the standard of perfection for efficiency in organization. It is amazing that in such a ship as the *Constitution* four hundred men could be cheerful and ready to fight after weeks and even months at sea.   They were crowded below the water line, without proper heat, plumbing, lighting, or ventilation, each man being allowed only twenty-eight inches by eight feet of space in which to sling his hammock against the beams overhead. Scurvy and other diseases were rampant. As many as seventy of the crew of the *Constitution* were on the sick list shortly before she fought the *Guerrière*. The food was wholesome for rugged men, but it was limited solely to salt beef, hard bread, dried peas, cheese, pork, and spirits.

Such conditions, however, had not destroyed the vigor of those hardy seamen of the *Constitution* when, on the 29th of December and within sight of the Brazilian coast, the lookout at the masthead sang out to Captain Bainbridge that a heavy ship was coming up under easy canvas. It turned out to be His Britannic Majesty's frigate *Java*, Captain Henry Lambert, who, like Carden, made the mistake of insisting upon a combat. His reasons were sounder than those of Dacres or Carden, however, for the *Java* was only a shade inferior to the *Constitution* in guns and carried as many men. In every respect they were so evenly matched that the test of battle could have no aftermath of extenuation.

The *Java* at once hastened in pursuit of the American ship which drew off the coast as though in flight, the real purpose being to get clear of the neutral Brazilian waters. The *Constitution* must have been a picture to stir the heart and kindle the imagination, her black hull heeling to the pressure of the tall canvas, the long rows of guns frowning from the open ports, while her bunting rippled a glorious defiance, with a commodore's pennant at the mainmast-head, the Stars and Stripes streaming from the mizzen peak and main-topgallant mast, and a Union Jack at the fore. The *Java* was adorned as bravely, and Captain Lambert had lashed an ensign in the rigging on the chance that his other colors might be shot away.

The two ships began the fray at what they called long range, which would be about a mile, and then swept onward to pass on opposite tacks. It was the favorite maneuver of trying to gain the weather gage, and while they were edging to windward a round shot smashed the wheel of the *Constitution* which so hampered her for the moment that Captain Lambert, handsomely taking advantage of the mishap, let the *Java* run past his enemy's stern and poured in a broadside which hit several of the American seamen. Both commanders displayed, in a high degree, the art of handling ships under sail as they luffed or wore and tenaciously jockeyed for position, while the gunners fought in the smoke that drifted between the frigates.

At length Captain Lambert became convinced that he had met his master at this agile style of warfare and determined to come to close quarters before the *Java* was fatally damaged. Her masts and yards were crashing to the deck and the slaughter among the crew was already appalling. Marines and seamen gathered in the gangways and upon the forecastle head to spring aboard the *Constitution*, but Captain Bainbridge drove his ship clear very shortly after the collision and continued to pound the *Java* to kindling-wood with his broadsides. The fate of the action was no longer in doubt. The British frigate was on fire, Captain Lambert was mortally wounded, and all her guns had been silenced. The *Constitution* hauled off to repair damages and stood back an hour later to administer the final blow. But the flag of the *Java* fluttered down, and the lieutenant in command surrendered.

The *Constitution* had again crushed the enemy with so little damage to herself that she was ready to continue her cruise, with a loss of only nine

killed and twenty-five wounded.   The *Java* was a
fine ship utterly destroyed, a sinking, dismasted
hulk, with a hundred and twenty-four of her men
dead or suffering from wounds.   It is significant to
learn that during six weeks at sea they had fired
but six practice broadsides, of blank cartridges, although there were many raw hands in the crew,
while the men of the *Constitution* had been incessantly drilled in firing until their team play was like
that of a football eleven.   There was no shooting
at random.   Under Hull and Bainbridge they had
been taught their trade, which was to lay the gun
on the target and shoot as rapidly as possible.

For the diminutive American navy, the year of
1812 came to its close with a record of success so
illustrious as to seem almost incredible.   It is more
dignified to refrain from extolling our own exploits
and to recall the effects of these sea duels upon the
minds of the people, the statesmen, and the press
of the England of that period.   Their outbursts of
wrathful humiliation were those of a maritime race
which cared little or nothing about the course of
the American war by land.   Theirs was the salty
tradition, virile and perpetual, which a century
later and in a friendlier guise was to create a Grand
Fleet which should keep watch and ward in the

misty Orkneys and hold the Seven Seas safe against the naval power of Imperial Germany. Then, as now, the English nation believed that its armed ships were its salvation.

It is easier to understand, bearing this in mind, why after the fight of the *Guerrière* the London *Times* indulged in such frenzied lamentations as these:

We witnessed the gloom which that event cast over high and honorable minds. . . . Never before in the history of the world did an English frigate strike to an American, and though we cannot say that Captain Dacres, under all circumstances, is punishable for this act, yet we do say there are commanders in the English navy who would a thousand times rather have gone down with their colors flying than to have set their fellow sailors so fatal an example.

Good God! that a few short months should have so altered the tone of British sentiments! Is it true, or is it not, that our navy was accustomed to hold the Americans in utter contempt? Is it true, or is it not, that the *Guerrière* sailed up and down the American coast with her name painted in large characters on her sails in boyish defiance of Commodore Rodgers? Would any captain, however young, have indulged such a foolish piece of vain-boasting if he had not been carried forward by the almost unanimous feeling of his associates?

We have since sent out more line-of-battle ships and heavier frigates.   Surely we must now mean to smother the American navy.   A very short time before the capture of the *Guerrière* an American frigate was an object of ridicule to our honest tars.   Now the prejudice is actually setting the other way and great pains seems to be taken by the friends of ministers to prepare the public for the surrender of a British seventy-four to an opponent lately so much contemned.

It was when the news reached England that the *Java* had been destroyed by the *Constitution* that indignation found a climax in the outcry of the *Pilot*, a foremost naval authority:

The public will learn, with sentiments which we shall not presume to anticipate, that a third British frigate has struck to an American.   This is an occurrence that calls for serious reflection, — this, and the fact stated in our paper of yesterday, that Lloyd's list contains notices of upwards of five hundred British vessels captured in seven months by the Americans.   Five hundred merchantmen and three frigates!   Can these statements be true; and can the English people hear them unmoved?   Any one who would have predicted such a result of an American war this time last year would have been treated as a madman or a traitor. He would have been told, if his opponents had condescended to argue with him, that long ere seven months had elapsed the American flag would have been swept from the seas, the contemptible navy of the United States annihilated, and their maritime arsenals rendered a heap of ruins. Yet down to this moment not a single American frigate has struck her flag. They insult and laugh at our want of enterprise and vigor. They leave their ports when they please and return to them when it suits their convenience; they traverse the Atlantic; they beset the West India Islands; they advance to the very chops of the Channel; they parade along the coasts of South America; nothing chases, nothing intercepts, nothing engages them but to yield them triumph.

It was to be taken for granted that England would do something more than scold about the audacity of the American navy. Even after the declaration of war her most influential men hoped that the repeal of the obnoxious Orders-in-Council might yet avert a solution of the American problem by means of the sword. There was hesitation to apply the utmost military and naval pressure, and New England was regarded with feelings almost friendly because of its opposition to an offensive warfare against Great Britain and an invasion of Canada.

Absorbed in the greater issue against Napoleon, England was nevertheless aroused to more vigorous action against the United States and devised strong blockading measures for the spring of 1813. Unable to operate against the enemy's ships in force

ISAAC HULL

Painting by J. W. Jarvis. In the City Hall, New York, owned by the Corporation. Reproduced by courtesy of the Municipal Art Commission of the City of New York.

WILLIAM BAINBRIDGE

Painting by J. W. Jarvis. In the City Hall, New York, owned by the Corporation. Reproduced by courtesy of the Municipal Art Commission of the City of New York.

ISAAC HULL

Painting by J. W. Jarvis. In the City Hall, New York, owned by the Corporation. Reproduced by courtesy of the Municipal Art Commission of the City of New York.

WILLIAM BAINBRIDGE

Painting by J. W. Jarvis. In the City Hall, New York, owned by the Corporation. Reproduced by courtesy of the Municipal Art Commission of the City of New York.

or to escape from ports which were sealed by vigilant squadrons, the American navy to a large extent was condemned to inactivity for the remainder of the war.   Occasional actions were fought and merit was justly won, but there was nothing like the glory of 1812, which shone undimmed by defeat and which gave to the annals of the nation one of its great chapters of heroic and masterful achievement.   It was singularly apt that the noble and victorious American frigates should have been called the *Constitution* and the *United States*.   They inspired a new respect for the flag with the stripes and the stars and for all that it symbolized.

CHAPTER VII

"DON'T GIVE UP THE SHIP!"

THE second year of the war by sea opened brilliantly enough to satisfy the American people, who
were now in a mood to expect too much of their
navy. In February the story of the *Wasp* and the
Frolic was repeated by two ships of precisely the
same class. The American sloop-of-war *Hornet* had
sailed to South America with the *Constitution* and
was detached to blockade, in the port of Bahia, the
British naval sloop *Bonne Citoyenne*, which con-
tained treasure to the amount of half a million
pounds in specie. Captain James Lawrence of the
Hornet sent in a challenge to fight, ship against
ship, pledging his word that the *Constitution* would
not interfere, but the British commander, perhaps
mindful of his precious cargo, declined the invitation. Instead of this, he sensibly sent word to a
great seventy-four at Rio de Janeiro, begging her
to come and drive the pestiferous *Hornet* away.

The British battleship arrived so suddenly that Captain Lawrence was compelled to dodge and flee in the darkness. By a close shave he gained the open sea and made off up the coast. For several weeks the *Hornet* idled to and fro, vainly seeking merchant prizes, and then off the Demerara River on February 24, 1813, she fell in with the British brig *Peacock*, that flew the royal ensign. The affair lasted no more than fifteen minutes. The *Peacock* was famous for shining brass work, spotless paint, and the immaculate trimness of a yacht, but her gunnery had been neglected, for which reason she went to the bottom in six fathoms of water with shot-holes in her hull and thirty-seven of her crew put out of action. The sting of the *Hornet* had been prompt and fatal. Captain Lawrence had only one man killed and two wounded, and his ship was as good as ever. Crowding his prisoners on board and being short of provisions and water, he set sail for a home port and anchored in New York harbor. He was in time to share with Bainbridge the carnival of salutes, processions, dinners, addresses of congratulation, votes of thanks, swords, medals, prize money, promotion — every possible tribute of an adoring and grateful people.

One of the awards bestowed upon Lawrence was

the command of the frigate *Chesapeake*. Among seamen she was rated an unlucky ship, and Lawrence was confidently expected to break the spell. Her old crew had left her after the latest voyage, which met with no success, and other sailors were reluctant to join her. Privateering had attracted many of them, and the navy was finding it difficult to recruit the kind of men it desired. Lawrence was compelled to sign on a scratch lot, some Portuguese, a few British, and many landlubbers. Given time to shake them together in hard service at sea, he would have made a smart crew of them no doubt, as Isaac Hull had done in five weeks with the men of the *Constitution*, but destiny ordered otherwise.

In the spring of 1813 the harbor of Boston was blockaded by the thirty-eight-gun British frigate *Shannon*, Captain Philip Vere Broke, who had been in this ship for seven years. In the opinion of Captain Mahan, "his was one of those cases where singular merit as an officer and an attention to duty altogether exceptional had not yet obtained opportunity for distinction. It would probably be safe to say that no more thoroughly efficient ship of her class had been seen in the British navy during the twenty years' war with France."

Captain Broke was justly confident in his own

leadership and in the efficiency of a ship's company, which had retained its identity of organization through so many years of his personal and energetic supervision. Indeed, the captain of the British flagship on the American station wrote: "The *Shannon's* men were trained and understood gunnery better than any men I ever saw." Every morning the men were exercised at training the guns and in the afternoon in the use of the broadsword, musket, and pike. Twice each week the crew fired at targets with great guns and musketry and the sailor who hit the bull's eye received a pound of tobacco. Without warning Captain Broke would order a cask tossed overboard and then suddenly order some particular gun to sink it. In brief, the *Shannon* possessed those qualities which had been notable in the victorious American frigates and which were lamentably deficient in the *Chesapeake*.

Lawrence's men were unknown to each other and to their officers, and they had never been to sea together. The last draft came aboard, in fact, just as the anchor was weighed and the *Chesapeake* stood out to meet her doom. Even most of her officers were new to the ship. They had no chance whatever to train or handle the rabble between

9

decks.   Now Captain Broke had been anxious to fight this American frigate as matching the *Shannon* in size and power.   He had already addressed to Captain Lawrence a challenge whose wording was a model of courtesy but which was provocative to the last degree.   A sailor of Lawrence's heroic temper was unlikely to avoid such a combat, stimulated as he was by the unbroken success of his own navy in duels between frigates.

On the first day of June, Captain Broke boldly ran into Boston harbor and broke out his flag in defiance of the *Chesapeake* which was riding at anchor as though waiting to go to sea.   Instantly accepting the invitation, Captain Lawrence hoisted colors, fired a gun, and mustered his crew.   In this ceremonious fashion, as gentlemen were wont to meet with pistols to dispute some point of honor, did the *Chesapeake* sail out to fight the waiting *Shannon*. The news spread fast and wide and thousands of people, as though they were bound to the theater, hastened to the heights of Malden, to Nahant, and to the headlands of Salem and Marblehead, in hopes of witnessing this famous sight.   They assumed that victory was inevitable.   Any other surmise was preposterous.

These eager crowds were cheated of the spectacle,

however, for the *Chesapeake* bore away to the eastward after rounding Boston Light and dropped hull down until her sails were lost in the summer haze, with the *Shannon* in her company as if they steered for some rendezvous. They were firing when last seen and the wind bore the echo of the guns, faint and far away. It was most extraordinary that three weeks passed before the people would believe the tidings of the disaster. A pilot who had left the *Chesapeake* at five o'clock in the afternoon reported that he was still near enough an hour later to see the two ships locked side by side, that a fearful explosion had happened aboard the *Chesapeake*, and that through a rift in the battle smoke he had beheld the British flag flying above the American frigate.

This report was confirmed by a fishing boat from Cape Ann and by the passengers in a coastwise packet, but the public doubted and still hoped until the newspapers came from Halifax with an account of the arrival of the *Chesapeake* as prize to the *Shannon* and of the funeral honors paid to the body of Captain James Lawrence. The tragic defeat came at an extremely dark moment of the war when almost every expectation had been disappointed and the future was clouded. Richard

Rush, the American diplomatist, wrote, recalling the event:

I remember — what American does not! — the first rumor of it. I remember the startling sensation. I remember at first the universal incredulity. I remember how the post-offices were thronged for successive days by anxious thousands; how collections of citizens rode out for miles on the highway, accosting the mail to catch something by anticipation. At last, when the certainty was known, I remember the public gloom; funeral orations and badges of mourning bespoke it. "Don't give up the ship" — the dying words of Lawrence — were on every tongue.

It was learned that the *Chesapeake* had followed the *Shannon* until five o'clock, when the latter luffed and showed her readiness to begin fighting. Lawrence was given the choice of position, with a westerly breeze, but he threw away this advantage, preferring to trust to his guns with a green crew rather than the complex and delicate business of maneuvering his ship under sail. He came bowling straight down at the *Shannon*, luffed in his turn, and engaged her at a distance of fifty yards. The breeze was strong and the nimble American frigate forged ahead more rapidly than Lawrence expected, so that presently her broadside guns had ceased to bear.

While Lawrence was trying to slacken headway and regain the desired position, the enemy's shot disabled his headsails, and the *Chesapeake* came up into the wind with canvas all a-flutter. It was a mishap which a crew of trained seamen might have quickly mended, but the frigate was taken aback — that is, the breeze drove her stern foremost toward the *Shannon* and exposed her to a deadly cannonade which the American gunners were unable to return. The hope of salvation lay in getting the ship under way again or in boarding the *Shannon*. It was in this moment that the battle was won and lost, for every gun of the British broadside was sweeping the American deck diagonally from stern to bow, while the marines in the tops of the *Shannon* picked off the officers and seamen of the *Chesapeake*, riddling them with musket balls. It was like the swift blast of a hurricane. Lawrence fell, mortally wounded. Ludlow, his first lieutenant, was carried below. The second lieutenant was stationed between decks, and the third forsook his post to assist those who were carrying Lawrence below to the gun deck. Not an officer remained on the spar deck and not a living man was left on the quarter deck when the *Chesapeake* drifted against the *Shannon* after four minutes of this infernal destruction. As the ships collided, Captain Broke dashed forward and shouted for boarders, leading them across to the American deck. No more than fifty men followed him and three hundred Yankee sailors should have been able to wipe the party out, but most of the *Chesapeake* crew were below, and, demoralized by lack of discipline and leadership, they refused to come up and stand the gaff. Brave resistance was made by the few who remained on deck and a dozen more followed the second lieutenant, George Budd, as he rushed up to rally a forlorn hope.

It was a desperate encounter while it lasted, and Captain Broke was slashed by a saber as he led a charge to clear the forecastle. Yet two minutes sufficed to clear the decks of the *Chesapeake*, and the few visible survivors were thrown down the hatchways. The guns ceased firing, and the crew below sent up a message of surrender. The frigates had drifted apart, leaving Broke and his seamen to fight without reinforcement, but before they came together again the day was won. This was the most humiliating phase of the episode, that a handful of British sailors and marines should have carried an American frigate by boarding.

It must not be inferred that the *Chesapeake*

inflicted no damage during the fifteen minutes of this famous engagement. Thirty-seven of the British boarding party were killed or wounded and the American marines — "leather-necks" then and "devil-dogs" now — fought in accordance with the spirit of a corps which had won its first laurels in the Revolution. Such broadsides as the *Chesapeake* was able to deliver were accurately placed and inflicted heavy losses. The victory cost the *Shannon* eighty-two men killed and wounded, while the American frigate lost one hundred and forty-seven of her crew, or more than one-third of her complement. Even in defeat the *Chesapeake* had punished the enemy far more severely than the *Constitution* had been able to do.

Lawrence lay in the cockpit, or hospital, when his men began to swarm down in confusion and leaderless panic. Still conscious, he was aware that disaster had overtaken them and he muttered again and again with his dying breath, "Don't give up the ship. Blow her up." Thus passed to an honorable fame an American naval officer of great gallantry and personal charm. Although he brought upon his country a bitter humiliation, the fact that he died sword in hand, his last thought for his flag and his service, has atoned for his faults of rashness and overconfidence. The odds were against him, and ill-luck smashed his chance of overcoming them. He was no more disgraced than Dacres when he surrendered the *Guerrière* to a heavier ship, or than Lambert, dying on his own deck, when he saw the colors of the *Java* hauled down.

The *Shannon* took her prize to Halifax, and when the news came back that the captain of the *Chesapeake* lay dead in a British port, the bronzed sea-dogs of the Salem Marine Society resolved to fetch his body home in a manner befitting his end. Captain George Crowninshield obtained permission from the Government to sail with a flag of truce for Halifax, and he equipped the brig *Henry* for the sad and solemn mission. Her crew was picked from among the shipmasters of Salem, some of them privateering skippers, every man of them a proven deep-water commander. It was such a crew as never before or since took a vessel out of an American port. When they returned to Salem with the remains of Captain Lawrence and Lieutenant Ludlow, the storied old seaport saw their funeral column pass through the quiet and crowded streets. The pall-bearers bore names to thrill American hearts today — Hull, Stewart, Bainbridge, Blakely, Creighton, and Parker, all captains of the navy. A Salem newspaper described the ceremonies simply and with an unconscious pathos:

The day was unclouded, as if no incident should be wanting to crown the mind with melancholy and woe — the wind from the same direction and the sea presented the same unruffled surface as was exhibited to our anxious view when on that memorable first day of July we saw the immortal Lawrence proudly conducting his ship to action. . . . The brig *Henry* containing the precious relics lay at anchor in the harbor. They were placed in barges and, preceded by a long procession of boats filled with seamen uniformed in blue jackets and trousers, with a blue ribbon on their hats bearing the motto of "Free Trade and Sailors' Rights," were rowed by minute strokes to the end of India Wharf, where the bearers were ready to receive the honored dead. From the time the boats left the brig until the bodies were landed, the United States brig *Rattlesnake* and the brig *Henry* alternately fired minute guns. . . . On arriving at the meeting-house the coffins were placed in the centre of the church by the seamen who rowed them ashore and who stood during the ceremony leaning upon them in an attitude of mourning. The church was decorated with cypress and evergreen, and the names of Lawrence and Ludlow appeared in gilded letters on the front of the pulpit.

It was wholly reasonable that the exploit of the *Shannon* should arouse fervid enthusiasm in the breast of every Briton. The wounds inflicted by Hull, Decatur, and Bainbridge still rankled, but they were now forgotten and the loud British boastings equaled all the tales of Yankee brag. A member of Parliament declared that the "action which Broke fought with the *Chesapeake* was in every respect unexampled. It was not — and he knew it was a bold assertion which he made — to be surpassed by any other engagement which graced the naval annals of Great Britain." Admiral Warren was still in a peevish humor at the hard knocks inflicted on the Royal Navy when he wrote, in congratulating Captain Broke: "At this critical moment you could not have restored to the British naval service the preëminence it has always preserved, or contradicted in a more forcible manner the foul aspersions and calumnies of a conceited, boasting enemy than by the brilliant act you have performed. The relation of such an event restores the history of ancient times and will do more good to the service than it is possible to conceive."

Captain Broke was made a baronet and received other honors and awards which he handsomely deserved, but the wound he had suffered at the head of his boarding party disabled him for further sea duty. If the influence of the *Constitution* and the *United States* was far-reaching in improving the efficiency of the American navy, it can be said also that the victory of the *Shannon* taught the British service the value of rigorous attention to gunnery and a highly trained and disciplined personnel.

American chagrin was somewhat softened a few weeks later when two very small ships, the *Enterprise* and the *Boxer*, met in a spirited combat off the harbor of Portland, Maine, like two bantam cocks, and the Britisher was beaten in short order on September 5, 1813. The *Enterprise* had been a Yankee schooner in the war with Tripoli but had been subsequently altered to a square rig and had received more guns and men to worry the enemy's privateers. The brig-of-war was a kind of vessel heartily disliked by seamen and now vanished from blue water. The immortal Boatswain Chucks of Marryat proclaimed that "they would certainly damn their inventor to all eternity" and that "their common, low names, 'Pincher,' 'Thrasher,' 'Boxer,' 'Badger,' and all that sort, are quite good enough for them."

Commanding the *Enterprise* was Captain William Burrows, twenty-eight years old, who had seen only a month of active service in the war.

Captain Samuel Blyth of the *Boxer* had worked his way up to this unimportant post after many years of arduous duty in the British navy. He might have declined a tussel with the *Enterprise* for his crew numbered only sixty-six men against a hundred and twenty, but he nailed his colors to the mainmast and remarked that they would never come down while there was any life in him.

The day was calm, the breeze fitful, and the little brigs drifted about each other until they lay within pistol shot. Then both loosed their broadsides, while the sailors shouted bravely, and both captains fell, Blyth killed instantly and Burrows mortally hurt but crying out that the flag must never be struck. There was no danger of this, for the *Enterprise* raked the British brig through and through until resistance was hopeless. Captain Blyth was as good as his word. He did not live to see his ensign torn down. Great hearts in little ships, these two captains were buried side by side in a churchyard which overlooks Casco Bay, and there you may read their epitaphs today.

The grim force of circumstances was beginning to alter the naval policy of the United States. Notwithstanding the dramatic successes, her flag was almost banished from the high seas by the close of

A FRIGATE OF 1812 UNDER SAIL

The *Constellation*, of which this is a photograph, is somewhat smaller than the *Constitution*, being rated at 38 guns as against 44 for the latter. In general appearance, however, and particularly in rig, the two types are very similar. Although the *Constellation* did not herself see action in the War of 1812, she is a good example of the heavily armed American frigate of that day — and the only one of them still to be seen at sea under sail within recent years. At the present time the *Constellation* lies moored at the pier of the Naval Training Station, Newport, R. I.

Photograph copyright by E. Muller, Jr., Inc., New York.

A FRIGATE OF 1812 UNDER SAIL.

The Constellation, of which this is a photograph, is somewhat smaller than the Constitution, being rated at 38 guns as against 44 for the latter. In general appearance, however, and particularly in rig, the two types are very similar. Although the Constellation did not herself see action in the War of 1812, she is a good example of the heavily armed American frigate of that day — and the only one of them still to be seen at sea under sail within recent years. At the present time the Constellation lies moored at the pier of the Naval Training Station, Newport, R. I.

Photograph copyright by E. Muller, Jr., Inc., New York.

the year 1813. The frigates *Constellation*, *United States*, and *Macedonian* were hemmed in port by the British blockade; the *Adams* and the *Constitution* were laid up for repairs; and the only formidable ships of war which roamed at large were the *President*, the *Essex*, and the *Congress*. The smaller vessels which had managed to slip seaward and which were of such immense value in destroying British commerce found that the system of convoying merchantmen in fleets of one hundred or two hundred sail had left the ocean almost bare of prizes. It was the habit of these convoys, however, to scatter as they neared their home ports, every skipper cracking on sail and the devil take the hindmost — a failing which has survived unto this day, and many a wrathful officer of an American cruiser or destroyer in the war against Germany could heartily echo the complaint of Nelson when he was a captain, "behaving as all convoys that ever I saw did, shamefully ill, and parting company every day."

This was the reason why American naval vessels and privateers left their own coasts and dared to rove in the English Channel, as Paul Jones had done in the *Ranger* a generation earlier. It was discovered that enemy merchantmen could be snapped up more easily within sight of their own shores than thousands of miles away. First to emphasize this fact in the War of 1812 was the naval brig *Argus*, Captain William H. Allen, which made a summer crossing and cruised for a month on end in the Irish Sea and in the chops of the Channel with a gorgeous recompense for her shameless audacity. England scolded herself red in the face while the saucy *Argus* captured twenty-seven ships and took her pick of their valuable cargoes. Her course could be traced by the blazing hulls that she left in her wake and this was how the British gun brig *Pelican* finally caught up with her.

Although the advantage of size and armament was with the *Pelican*, it was to be expected that the *Argus* would prove more than a match for her. The American commander, Captain Allen, had played a distinguished part in several of the most famous episodes of the navy. As third lieutenant of the *Chesapeake*, in 1807, he had picked up a live coal in the cook's galley, held it in his fingers, and so fired the only gun discharged against the *Leopard* in that inglorious surprise and surrender. As first officer of the frigate *United States* he received credit for the splendid gunnery which had overwhelmed the *Macedonian*, and he enjoyed the glory of bringing the prize to port. It was as a reward of merit that he was given command of the *Argus*. Alas, in this fight off the coast of Wales he lost both his ship and his life, and England had scored again. There was no ill-luck this time — nothing to plead in excuse. The American brig threw away a chance of victory because her shooting was amazingly bad, and instead of defending the deck with pistol, pike, and musket, when the boarders came over the bow the crew lowered the flag.

It was an early morning fight, on August 14, 1813, in which Captain Allen had his leg shot off within five minutes after the two brigs had engaged. He refused to be taken below, but loss of blood soon made him incapable of command, and presently his first lieutenant was stunned by a grapeshot which grazed his scalp. The ship was well sailed, however, and gained a position for raking the *Pelican* in deadly fashion, but the shot went wild and scarcely any harm was done. The British captain chose his own range and methodically made a wreck of the *Argus* in twenty minutes of smashing fire, working around her at will while not a gun returned his broadsides. Then he sheered close and was prepared to finish it on the deck of the *Argus* when she surrendered with twenty-three of her crew out of action. The *Pelican* was so little punished that only two men were killed. The officer left in command of the *Argus* laid this unhappy conclusion to "the superior size and metal of our opponent, and the fatigue which the crew underwent from a very rapid succession of prizes." There were those on board who blamed it to the casks of Oporto wine which had been taken out of the latest prize and which the sailors had secretly tapped. Honesty is the best policy, even in dealing with an enemy. The affair of the *Argus* and the *Pelican* was not calculated to inflate Yankee pride.

To balance this, however, came two brilliant actions by small ships. The new *Peacock*, named for the captured British brig, under Captain Lewis Warrington, stole past the blockade of New York. Off the Florida coast on the 29th of April she sighted a convoy and attacked the escort brig of eighteen guns, the *Epervier*. In this instance the behavior of the American vessel and her crew was supremely excellent and not a flaw could be found. They hulled the British brig forty-five times and made a shambles of her deck and did it with the loss of one man.

Even more sensational was the last cruise of the *Wasp*, Captain Johnston Blakely, which sailed from Portsmouth, New Hampshire, in May and roamed the English Channel to the dismay of all honest British merchantmen. The brig-of-war *Reindeer* endeavored to put an end to her career but nineteen minutes sufficed to finish an action in which the *Wasp* slaughtered half the British crew and thrice repelled boarders. This was no light task, for as Michael Scott, the British author of *Tom Cringle's Log*, candidly expressed it:

In the field, or grappling in mortal combat on the blood-slippery deck of an enemy's vessel, a British soldier or sailor is the bravest of the brave. No soldier or sailor of any other country, saving and excepting those damned Yankees, can stand against them. . . . I don't like Americans. I never did and never shall like them. I have no wish to eat with them, drink with them, deal with or consort with them in any way; but let me tell the whole truth, — *nor fight* with them, were it not for the laurel to be acquired by overcoming an enemy so brave, determined, and alert, and every way so worthy of one's steel as they have always proved.

Refitting in a French port, the dashing Blakely took the *Wasp* to sea again and encountered a convoy in charge of a huge, lumbering ship of the line. Nothing daunted, the *Wasp* flitted in among the timid merchant ships and snatched a valuable prize

10

laden with guns and military stores. Attempting to bag another, she was chased away by the indignant seventy-four and winged it in search of other quarry until she sighted four strange sails. Three of them were British war brigs in hot pursuit of a Yankee privateer, and Johnston Blakely was delighted to play a hand in the game. He selected his opponent, which happened to be the *Avon*, and overtook her in the darkness of evening. Before a strong wind they foamed side by side, while the guns flashed crimson beneath the shadowy gleam of tall canvas. Thus they ran for an hour and a half, and then the *Avon* signaled that she was beaten, with five guns dismounted, forty-two men dead or wounded, seven feet of water in the hold, the magazine flooded, and the spars and rigging almost destroyed.

Blakely was about to send a crew aboard when another hostile brig, forsaking the agile Yankee privateer, came up to help the *Avon*. The *Wasp* was perfectly willing to take on this second adversary, but just then a third British ship loomed through the obscurity, and the ocean seemed a trifle overpopulated for safety. Blakely ran off before the wind, compelled to abandon his prize. The *Avon*, however, was so badly battered that she went to the bottom before the wounded seamen could be removed from her. Thence the *Wasp* went to Madeira and was later reported as spoken near the Cape Verde Islands, but after that she vanished from blue water, erased by some tragic fate whose mystery was never solved. To the port of missing ships she carried brave Blakely and his men after a meteoric career which had swept her from one victory to another.

Of the frigates, only three saw action during the last two years of the war, and of these the *President* and the *Essex* were compelled to strike to superior forces of the enemy. The *Constitution* was lucky enough to gain the open sea in December, 1814, and fought her farewell battle with the frigate *Cyane* and the sloop-of-war *Levant* on the 20th of February. In this fight Captain Charles Stewart showed himself a gallant successor to Hull and Bainbridge. Together the two British ships were stronger than the *Constitution*, but Stewart cleverly hammered the one and then the other and captured both. Honor was also due the plucky little *Levant*, which, instead of taking to her heels, stood by to assist her larger comrade like a terrier at the throat of a wolf. It is interesting to note that the captains, English and American, had received word that peace had been declared, but without official confirmation they preferred to ignore it. The spirit which lent to naval warfare the spirit of the duel was too strong to let the opportunity pass.

The *President* was a victim of a continually increased naval strength by means of which Great Britain was able to strangle the seafaring trade and commerce of the United States as the war drew toward its close. Captain Decatur, who had taken command of this frigate, remarked "the great apprehension and danger" which New York felt, in common with the entire seaboard, and the anxiety of the city government that the crew of the ship should remain for defense of the port. Coastwise navigation was almost wholly suspended, and thousands of sloops and schooners feared to undertake voyages to Philadelphia, Baltimore, or Charleston. Instead of these, canvas-covered wagons struggled over the poor highways in continuous streams between New England and the Southern coast towns. This awkward result of the blockade moved the sense of humor of the Yankee rhymsters who placarded the wagons with such mottoes as "Free Trade and Oxen's Rights" and parodied *Ye Mariners of England* with the lines:

Ye wagoners of Freedom
Whose chargers chew the cud,
Whose wheels have braved a dozen years
The gravel and the mud;
Your glorious hawbucks yoke again
To take another jag,
And scud through the mud
Where the heavy wheels do drag,
Where the wagon creak is long and low
And the jaded oxen lag.

Columbia needs no wooden walls,
No ships where billows swell;
Her march is like a terrapin's,
Her home is in her shell.
To guard her trade and sailor's rights,
In woods she spreads her flag.

Such ribald nonsense, however, was unfair to a navy which had done magnificently well until smothered and suppressed by sheer weight of numbers. It was in January, 1815, that Captain Decatur finally sailed out of New York harbor in the hope of taking the *President* past the blockading division which had been driven offshore by a heavy northeast gale. The British ships were struggling back to their stations when they spied the Yankee frigate off the southern coast of Long Island. It was a stern chase, Decatur with a hostile squadron at his heels and unable to turn and fight because the odds were hopeless. The frigate *Endymion* was faster than her consorts and, as she came up alone, the *President* delayed to exchange broadsides before fleeing again with every sail set. Her speed had been impaired by stranding as she came out past Sandy Hook, else she might have outfooted the enemy. But soon the *Pomone* and the *Tenedos*, frigates of the class of the *Shannon* and the *Guerrière*, were in the hunt. Decatur was cornered, but his guns were served until a fifth of the crew were disabled, the ship was crippled, and a force fourfold greater than his own was closing in to annihilate him at its leisure. "I deemed it my duty to surrender," said he, and a noble American frigate, more formidable than the *Constitution*, was added to the list of the Royal Navy.

CHAPTER VIII

THE LAST CRUISE OF THE ESSEX

THE last cruise of the *Essex* frigate, although an ill-fated one, makes a story far less mournful than that of the *President*. She was the first man-of-war to display the American flag in the wide waters of the Pacific. Her long and venturesome voyage is still regarded as one of the finest achievements of the navy, and it made secure the fame of Captain David Porter. The *Essex* has a peculiar right to be held in affectionate memory, apart from the very gallant manner of her ending, because into her very timbers were builded the faith and patriotism of the people of the New England seaport which had framed and launched her as a loan to the nation in an earlier time of stress.

At the end of the eighteenth century France had been the maritime enemy more hotly detested than England, and unofficial war existed with the "Terrible Republic." This situation was foreshadowed as early as 1798 by James McHenry, Secretary of War, when he indignantly announced to Congress: "To forbear under such circumstances from taking naval and military measures to secure our trade, defend our territories in case of invasion, and to prevent or suppress domestic insurrection would be to offer up the United States a certain prey to France and exhibit to the world a sad spectacle of national degradation and imbecility."

Congress thereupon resolved to build two dozen ships which should teach France to mend her manners on the high seas, but the Treasury was too poor to pay the million dollars which this modest navy was to cost. Subscription lists were therefore opened in several shipping towns, and private capital advanced the funds to put the needed frigates afloat. The *Essex* was promptly contributed by Salem, and the advertisement of the master builder is brave and resonant reading:

To Sons of Freedom! All true lovers of Liberty of your Country! Step forth and give your assistance in building the frigate to oppose French insolence and piracy. Let every man in possession of a white oak tree be ambitious to be foremost in hurrying down the timber to Salem where the noble structure is to be fabricated to maintain your rights upon the seas and make the name of America respected among the

nations of the world. Your largest and longest trees
are wanted, and the arms of them for knees and rising
timber. Four trees are wanted for the keel which
altogether will measure 146 feet in length and hew
sixteen inches square.

The story of the building of the *Essex* is that of
an aroused and reliant people.   The great timbers
were cut in the wood lots of the towns near by and
were hauled through the snowy streets of Salem
on ox-sleds while the people cheered them as they
passed.   The *Essex* was a Salem ship from keel to
truck.   Her cordage was made in three ropewalks.
Captain Jonathan Haraden, the most famous Salem privateersman of the Revolution, made the
rigging for the mainmast in his loft.   The sails
were cut from duck woven for the purpose in the
mill on Broad Street and the ironwork was forged
by Salem shipsmiths. When the huge hempen
cables were ready to be conveyed to the frigate, the
workmen hoisted them upon their shoulders and in
procession marched to the music of fife and drum.
In 1799, six months after the oak timbers had been
standing trees, the *Essex* slid from the stocks into the
harbor of old Salem.   She was the handsomest and
fastest American frigate of her day and when turned
over to the Government, she cost what seemed at

that day the very considerable amount of seventy-five thousand dollars.

Peace was patched up with France, however, and the *Essex* was compelled to pursue more hum-drum paths, now in the Indian Ocean and again with the Mediterranean squadron, until war with England began in 1812. It was intended that Captain Porter should rendezvous with the *Constitution* and the *Hornet* in South American waters for a well-planned cruise against British commerce, but other engagements detained Bainbridge, notably his encounter with the *Java*, and so they missed each other by a thousand miles or so. Since he had no means of communication, it was characteristic of Porter to conclude to strike out for himself instead of wandering about in an uncertain search for his friends.

Porter conceived the bold plan of rounding the Horn and playing havoc with the British whaling fleet. This adventure would take him ten thousand miles from the nearest American port, but he reckoned that he could capture provisions enough to feed his crew and supplies to refit the ship. As a raid there was nothing to match this cruise until the *Alabama* ran amuck among the Yankee clippers and whaling barks half a century later. It was the wrong time of year to brave the foul weather of Cape Horn, however, and the *Essex* was battered and swept by one furious gale after another. But at last she won through, stout ship that she was, and her weary sailors found brief respite in the harbor of Valparaiso on March 14, 1813. Thence Porter headed up the coast, disguising the trim frigate so that she looked like a lubberly, high-pooped Spanish merchantman.

The luck of the navy was with the American captain for, as he went poking about the Galapagos Islands, he surprised three fine, large British whaling ships, all carrying guns and too useful to destroy. To one of them, the *Georgiana*, he shifted more guns, put a crew of forty men aboard under Lieutenant John Downes, ran up the American flag, and commissioned his prize as a cruiser. The other two he also manned — and now behold him, if you please, sailing the Pacific with a squadron of four good ships! Soon he ran down and captured two British letter-of-marque vessels, well armed and in fighting trim, and in a trice he had not a squadron but a fleet under his command, seven ships in all, mounting eighty guns and carrying three hundred and forty men and eighty prisoners. Two of these prizes he discovered to be crammed to the hatches with cordage, paint, tar, canvas, and fresh provisions. The list could not have been more acceptable if Captain David Porter himself had signed the requisition in the New York Navy Yard.

Lieutenant Downes was now sent off cruising by himself, and so well did he profit by his captain's example and precepts that in a little while he had bagged a squadron of his own, three ships with twenty-seven guns and seventy-five men. When he rejoined the flagship in a harbor of the mainland, Porter rewarded him by calling his cruiser the *Essex, Junior,* promoting him to the rank of commander, and increasing his armament. They then resumed cruising in two squadrons, finding more British ships and sending them into the neutral harbor of Valparaiso or home to the United States with precious cargoes of whale oil and bone. Within a few months he swept the Southern Pacific almost clean of British merchantmen, whalers, and privateers. Winter coming on, Porter then sailed to the pleasant Marquesas Islands and laid the *Essex* up for a thorough overhauling. The enemy had furnished all needful supplies and even the money to pay the wages of the officers and crew.

Fit for sea again, the *Essex* and the *Essex, Junior,*

betook themselves to Valparaiso where they received information that the thirty-six-gun frigate *Phœbe* of the British navy was earnestly looking for them. She had been sent out from England to proceed to the northwest American coast and destroy the fur station at the mouth of the Columbia River. At Rio de Janeiro Captain Hillyar had heard reports of the ravages of the *Essex* and he considered it his business to hunt down this defiant Yankee. To make sure of success, he took the sloop-of-war *Cherub* along with him and, doubling the Horn, they made straight for Valparaiso. David Porter got wind of the pursuit but assumed that the *Phœbe* was alone. He made no attempt to avoid a meeting but on the contrary rather courted a fight with his old friend Hillyar, whom he had known socially on the Mediterranean station. For an officer of Porter's temper and training the capture of British whalers was a useful but by no means glorious employment. He believed the real vocation of a frigate of the American navy was to engage the enemy.

The *Phœbe* and the *Cherub* sailed into the Chilean roadstead in February, 1814, and found the *Essex* there. As Captain Hillyar was passing in to seek an anchorage, the mate of a British merchantman climbed aboard to tell him that the *Essex* was unprepared for attack and could be taken with ease. Her officers had given a ball the night before in honor of the Spanish dignitaries of Valparaiso, and the decks were still covered with awnings and gay with bunting and flags. Reluctant to forego such a tempting opportunity, Captain Hillyar ran in and luffed his frigate within a few yards of the Essex. To his disappointed surprise, the American fighting ship was ready for action on the instant. Though the punctilious restraints of a neutral port should have compelled them to delay battle, Porter was vigilant and took no chances. The liberty parties had been recalled from shore, the decks had been cleared, the gunners were sent to quarters with matches lighted, and the boarders were standing by the hammock nettings with cutlasses gripped. Making the best of this unexpected turn of events, the English captain shouted a greeting to David Porter and politely conveyed his compliments, adding that his own ship was also ready for action. So close were the two frigates at this moment that the jib-boom of the *Phœbe* hung over the bulwarks of the *Essex*, and Porter called out sharply that if so much as a rope was touched he would reply with a broadside. The urbane Captain Hillyar, perceiving his disadvantage, exclaimed, "I had no intention of coming so near you. I am very sorry indeed." With that he moved his ship to a respectful distance. Later he had a chat with Captain Porter ashore and, when asked if he intended to maintain the neutrality of the port, made haste to protest, "Sir, you have been so careful to observe the rules that I feel myself bound in honor to do the same."

After a few days the *Phœbe* and the *Cherub* left the harbor and watchfully waited outside, enforcing a strict blockade and determined to render the *Essex* harmless unless she should choose to sally out and fight. David Porter was an intrepid but not a reckless sailor. He had the faster frigate but he had unluckily changed her battery from the long guns to the more numerous but shorter range carronades. He was not afraid to risk a duel with the *Phœbe* even with this handicap in armament, but the sloop-of-war *Cherub* was a formidable vessel for her size and the *Essex, Junior*, which was only a converted merchantman, was of small account in a hammer-and-tongs action between naval ships.

For his part, Captain Hillyar had no intention of letting the Yankee frigate escape him. "He was an old disciple of Nelson," observes Mahan, "fully imbued with the teaching that the achievement of success and not personal glory must dictate action. Having a well established reputation for courage and conduct, he intended to leave nothing to the chances of fortune which might decide a combat between equals. He therefore would accept no provocation to fight without the *Cherub*. His duty was to destroy the *Essex* with the least possible loss."

Porter endured this vexatious situation for six weeks and then, learning that other British frigates were on his trail, determined to escape to the open sea. This decision involved waiting for the most favorable moment of wind and weather, but Porter found his hand forced on the 28th of March by a violent southerly gale which swept over the exposed bay of Valparaiso and dragged the *Essex* from her anchorage. One of her cables parted while the crew struggled to get sail on her. As she drifted seaward, Porter decided to seize the emergency and take the long chance of running out to windward of the *Phœbe* and the *Cherub*. He therefore cut the other cable, and the *Essex* plunged into the wind under single-reefed topsails to claw past the headland. Just as she was about to clear it, a whistling squall carried away the maintopmast.

This accident was a grave disaster, for the disabled frigate was now unable either to regain a refuge in the bay or to win her way past the British ship.

As a last resort Captain Porter turned and ran along the coast, within pistol shot of it, far inside the three-mile limit of neutral water, and came to an anchor about three miles north of the city. Captain Hillyar had no legal right to molest him, but in his opinion the end justified the means and he resolved to attack. Deliberately the *Phœbe* and *Cherub* selected their stations and, late in this stormy afternoon, bombarded the crippled *Essex* without mercy. Porter with his carronades was unable to repay the damage inflicted by the broadsides of the longer guns, nor could he handle his ship to close in and retrieve the day in the desperate game of boarding. He tried this ultimate venture, nevertheless, and let go his cables. But the ship refused to move ahead. Her sheets, tacks, and halliards had been shot away. The canvas was hanging loose.

Porter's guns were by no means silent, however, even in this hopeless situation, and few crews have died harder or fought more grimly than these seamen of the *Essex*. Among them was a little midshipman, wounded but still at his post, a mere child of thirteen years whose name was David Farragut. His fortune it was to link those early days of the American navy with a period half a century later when he won his renown as the greatest of American admirals.

In many a New England seaport were told the tales of this last fight of the *Essex* until they became almost legendary — of Seaman John Ripley, who cried, after losing his leg, "Farewell, boys, I can be of no more use to you," and thereupon flung himself overboard out of a bow port; of James Anderson, who died encouraging his comrades to fight bravely in defense of liberty; of Benjamin Hazen, who dressed himself in a clean shirt and jerkin, told his messmates that he could never submit to being taken prisoner by the English and forthwith leaped into the sea and was drowned. Such incidents help us to descry, amid the smoke and slaughter of that desperate encounter, the spirit of the gallant David Porter. Never was the saying, "It's not the ships but the men in them," better exemplified. To Porter was granted greatness in defeat, a lot that comes to few.

For two hours he and his men endured such dreadful punishment as not many ships have suffered. Again he attempted to work his way nearer the enemy, until he had not enough men left unhurt to serve the guns or to haul at the pitifully splintered spars. In the last extremity, Porter made an effort to destroy his vessel and to save her people from captivity by letting the *Essex* drive ashore. A kedge anchor was let go, and a dozen sailors tramped around the capstan while the chantey man piped up a tune, but again fortune seemed against him for the hawser snapped, and the wind began to blow the frigate into deeper water. What happened then is best recalled in the simple words of Captain David Porter himself:

I now sent for the officers of division to consult them and what was my surprise to find only acting Lieutenant Stephen Decatur M'Knight remaining. . . . I was informed that the cockpit, the steerage, the wardroom, and the berth deck could contain no more wounded, that the wounded were killed while the surgeons were dressing them, and that if something was not speedily done to prevent it, the ship would soon sink from the number of shot holes in her bottom. On sending for the carpenter he informed me that all his crew had been killed or wounded.

The enemy, from the impossibility of reaching him with our carronades and the little apprehension that was excited by our fire, which had now become much slackened, was enabled to take aim at us as at a target; his shot never missed our hull and my ship was cut up in a manner which was perhaps never before witnessed;

in fine, I saw no hope of saving her, and at twenty minutes after 6 P.M. I gave the painful order to strike the colors. Seventy-five men including officers were all that remained of my whole crew after the action, many of them severely wounded, some of whom have since died.

The enemy still continued his fire and my brave, though unfortunate companions were still falling about me. I directed an opposite gun to be fired to show them we intended no further resistance but they did not desist. Four men were killed at my side and others at different parts of the ship. I now believed he intended to show us no quarter, that it would be as well to die with my flag flying as struck, and was on the point of again hoisting it when about ten minutes after hauling down the colors he ceased firing.

. . . We have been unfortunate but not disgraced — the defense of the *Essex* has not been less honorable to her officers and crew than the capture of an equal force; and I now consider my situation less unpleasant than that of Captain Hillyar, who in violation of every principle of honor and generosity, and regardless of the rights of nations, attacked the *Essex* in her crippled state within pistol shot of a neutral shore, when for six weeks I had daily offered him fair and honorable combat on terms greatly to his advantage.

The behavior of Captain Hillyar after the surrender, however, was most humane and courteous, and lapse of time has dispelled somewhat of the bitterness of the American opinion of him. If he

was not as chivalrous as his Yankee foemen had
expected, it must be remembered that there was a
heavy grudge and a long score to pay in the havoc
wrought among British merchantmen and whalers
and that in those days the rights of South American
neutrals were rather lightly regarded.

CHAPTER IX

VICTORY ON LAKE CHAMPLAIN

SPECTACULAR as were the exploits of the American navy on the sea, they were of far less immediate consequence in deciding the destinies of the war than were the naval battles fought on fresh water between hastily improvised squadrons. On Lake Erie Perry's victory had recovered a lost empire and had made the West secure against invasion. Macdonough's handful of little vessels on Lake Champlain compelled the retreat of ten thousand British veterans of Wellington's campaigns who had marched down from Canada with every promise of crushing American resistance. This was the last and most formidable attempt on the part of the enemy to conquer territory and to wrest a decision by means of a sustained offensive. Its collapse marked the beginning of the end, and such events as the capture of Washington and the battle of New Orleans were in the nature of episodes.

That September day of 1814, when Macdonough won his niche in the naval hall of fame,
was also the climax and the conclusion of the
long struggle of the American armies on the
northern frontier, a confused record of defeat,
vacillation, and crumbling forces, which was redeemed towards the end by troops who had
learned how to fight and by new leaders who
restored the honor of the flag at Chippawa and
Lundy's Lane. Although the ambitious attempts
against Canada, so often repeated, were so much
wasted effort until the very end, they ceased to
be inglorious. The tide turned in the summer
of 1814 with the renewal of the struggle for the
Niagara region where the British had won a
foothold upon American soil.

In command of a vigorous and disciplined American army was General Jacob Brown, that stout-
hearted volunteer who had proved his worth when
the enemy landed at Sackett's Harbor. He was
not a professional soldier but his troops had been
trained and organized by Winfield Scott who was
now a brigadier. After two years of dismal reverses, the United States was learning how to wage
war. Incompetency was no longer the badge of
high military rank. A general was supposed to

know something about his trade and to have a will of his own.

With thirty-five hundred men, Jacob Brown made a resolute advance to find and join battle with the British forces of General Riall which garrisoned the forts of St. George's, Niagara, Erie, Queenston, and Chippawa. Early in the morning of July 3, 1814, the American troops in two divisions crossed the river and promptly captured Fort Erie. They then pushed ahead fifteen miles until they encountered the British defensive line on the Chippawa River where it flows into the Niagara.

The field was like a park, with open, grassy spaces and a belt of woodland which served as a green curtain to screen the movements of both armies. Riall boldly assumed the offensive, although he was aware that he had fewer men. His instructions intimated that liberties might be taken with the Americans which would seem hazardous "to a military man unacquainted with the character of the enemy he had to contend with, or with the events of the last two campaigns on that frontier." The deduction was unflattering but very much after the fact.

The British attack was unlooked for. It was the Fourth of July and in celebration Winfield

Scott had given his men the best dinner that the commissary could supply and was marching them into a meadow in the cool of the summer afternoon for drill and review. The celebration, however, was interrupted by firing and confusion among the militia who happened to be in front, and Scott rushed his brigade forward to take the brunt of the heavy assault. General Jacob Brown rode by at a gallop, waving his hat and cheerily shouting, "You will have a battle." He was hurrying to bring up his other forces, but meanwhile Scott's column crossed a bridge at the double-quick and faced the enemy's batteries.

Exposed, taken by surprise, and outnumbered, Winfield Scott and his regiments were nevertheless equal to the occasion. A battalion was sent to cover one flank in the dense woodland, while the main body drove straight for the columns of British infantry and then charged with bayonets at sixty paces. The American ranks were steady and unbroken although they were pelted with musketry fire, and they smashed a British counter-charge by three regiments before it gained momentum. Handsomely fought and won, it was not a decisive battle and might be called no more than a skirmish but its significance was highly important, for at

Chippawa there was displayed a new spirit in the American army.

Riall retreated with his red-coated regulars to a stronger line at Queenston, while Jacob Brown was sending anxious messages to Commodore Chauncey begging him to use his fleet in coöperation and so break the power of the enemy in Upper Canada. "For God's sake, let me see you," he implored. But again the American ships on Lake Ontario failed to seize an opportunity, and in this instance Chauncey's inactivity dismayed not only General Brown but also the Government at Washington. The fleet remained at Sackett's Harbor with excuses which appeared inadequate: certain changes were being made among the officers and crews, and again "the squadron had been prevented being earlier fitted for sea in consequence of the delay in obtaining blocks and iron-work." Chauncey subsequently fell ill, which may have had something to do with his lapse of energy. The whole career of this naval commander on Lake Ontario had disappointed expectations, even though the Secretary had commended his "zeal, talent, constancy, courage, and prudence of the highest order." The trouble was that Chauncey let slip one chance after another to win the control of Lake Ontario in

pitched battle. Always too intent on building
more ships instead of fighting with those he had,
he is therefore not remembered in the glorious
companionship of Perry and Macdonough.

This failure to act at the moment when Jacob
Brown was so valiantly endeavoring to wrest from
the British the precious Niagara peninsula was
responsible for the desperate and inconclusive
battle of Lundy's Lane. Winfield Scott frankly
blamed the unsuccessful result upon the freedom
with which the British troops and supplies were
moved on Lake Ontario. For ten days Jacob
Brown had remained in a painful state of suspense
and perplexity, until finally the word came that
nobody knew when the American fleet would sail.
As he had feared, the British command, able to
move its troops unmolested across the lake,
planned to attack him in the rear and to cut
his communications on the New York side of the
Niagara River.   For this purpose two enemy brigs
were filled with troops and were sent over to Fort
Niagara with more to follow.

It was to parry this threat that Brown moved
his forces and brought about the clash at Lundy's
Lane. "As it appeared," he explained, "that the
enemy with his increased strength was about to

avail himself of the hazard under which our baggage and stores were on our side of the Niagara, I conceived the most effectual method of recalling him from the object was to put myself in motion towards Queenston. General Scott with his brigade were accordingly put in march on the road leading thither."

The action was fought about a mile back from the torrent of the Niagara, below the Falls, where the by-road known as Lundy's Lane joined the main road running parallel with the river. Here Scott's column came suddenly upon a force of British redcoats led by General Drummond. Scott hesitated to attack, because the odds were against his one brigade, but, fearing the effect of a retreat on the divisions behind him, he sent word to Brown that he would hold his ground and try to turn the enemy's left toward the Niagara. It was late in the day and the sun had almost set. Gradually Scott forced the British wing back, and Brown threw in reinforcements until the engagement became general. The fight continued furious even after darkness fell and never have men employed in the business of killing each other shown courage more stubborn. Both sides were equally determined and they fought until exhaustion literally compelled a halt.

Later in the evening fresh troops were hurled in on both sides, and they were at it again with the same impetuosity. A small hill, over which ran Lundy's Lane, was the goal the Americans fought for. They finally stormed it, "in so determined a manner," reported the enemy, "that our artillery men were bayoneted in the act of loading and the muzzles of the enemy's guns were advanced within a few yards of ours." Back and forth flowed the tide of battle in bloody waves, until midnight. Then sullenly and in good order the Americans retired three miles to camp at Chippawa. Next day the enemy resumed the position and held it unattacked.

It is fair to call Lundy's Lane a drawn battle. The casualties were something more than eight hundred for each side, and the troops engaged were about twenty-five hundred Americans and a like number of British. Both the shattered columns soon retired behind strong defenses. General Drummond led the British troops into camp at Niagara Falls, and General Ripley, in temporary command of the American brigades, Scott and Brown having been wounded, occupied the unfinished works of Fort Erie, on the Canadian side, just where the waters of Lake Erie enter the Niagara River.

The British determined to bombard these walls and intrenchments with heavy guns and then carry them by infantry assault. But this plan failed disastrously. On the 15th of August the British charged in three columns the bastions and batteries only to be savagely repulsed at every point with a loss of nine hundred men killed, wounded, or prisoners, while the defenders had only eighty-five casualties. Then Drummond settled down to besiege the place and succeeded in making it so uncomfortable that Jacob Brown, now recovered from his wound, organized a sortie in force which was made on the 17th of September. In the action which followed, the British batteries were overwhelmed and the American militia displayed magnificent steadiness and valor. Jacob Brown proudly informed the Governor of New York that "the militia of New York have redeemed their character — they behaved gallantly. Of those called out by the last requisition, fifteen hundred have crossed the state border to our support. This reinforcement has been of immense importance to us; it doubled our effective strength, and their good conduct cannot but have the happiest effect upon our nation."

This bold stroke ended the Niagara campaign.

The British fell back, and the American army was in no condition for pursuit. In ten weeks Jacob Brown had fought four engagements without defeat and, barring the battle of New Orleans, his brief campaign was the one operation of the land war upon which Americans could look back with any degree of satisfaction.

The scene now shifted to Lake Champlain. The main work was the building up of an army to resist the menacing preparations for a British invasion from Montreal. Among the new American generals who had gained promotion by merit instead of favor was George Izard, trained in the military schools of England and Prussia, and an aide to Alexander Hamilton during his command of the army of the United States. Izard had been sent to Plattsburg in May, 1814, on the very eve of the great British campaign, and found everything in a deplorable state of unreadiness and inefficiency. While he was manfully struggling with these difficulties, Secretary Armstrong directed him to send four thousand of his men to the assistance of Jacob Brown on the Niagara front. General Izard obediently and promptly set out, although the defense of Lake Champlain was thereby deprived of this large body of troops. The expedition was

almost barren of results, however, and at a time
when every trained soldier was needed to oppose
the march of the British veterans, Izard was at
Fort Erie, idle, waiting to build winter quarters
and writing to the War Department: "I confess
I am greatly embarrassed. At the head of the
most efficient army the United States have possessed during this war, much must be expected of
me; and yet I can discern no object which can be
achieved at this point worthy of the risk which will
attend its attempt."

Izard had already predicted that the withdrawal
of his forces from Plattsburg would leave north-
eastern New York at the mercy of the British and
he spoke the truth. No sooner had his divisions
started westward than the British army, ten thousand strong, under General Prevost, crossed the
frontier and marched rapidly toward the Saranac
River and then straight on to Plattsburg. Possession of this trading town the British particularly
desired because through it passed an enormous
amount of illicit traffic with Canada. Both Izard
and Prevost agreed in the statement that the
British army was almost entirely fed on supplies
drawn from New York and Vermont by way of
Lake Champlain. "Two thirds of the army in

Canada are supplied with beef by American con-
tractors," wrote Prevost, and there were not
enough highways to accommodate the herds of
cattle which were driven across the border.

To protect this source of supply by conquering
the region was the task assigned the splendid army
of British regulars who had fought under Wellington. The conclusion of the Peninsular campaign
had released them for service in America, and England was now able for the first time to throw her
military strength against the feeble forces of the
United States.   It was announced as the intention
of the British Government to take and hold the
lakes, from Champlain to Erie, as territorial waters
and a permanent barrier. To oppose the large
and seasoned army which was to effect these proj-
ects, there was an American force of only fifteen
hundred men, led by Brigadier General Alexander
Macomb.   All he could do was to try to hold the
defensive works at Plattsburg and to send forward
small skirmishing parties to annoy the British
army which advanced in solid column, without
taking the trouble to deploy.

On the 6th of September Sir George Prevost with
his army reached Plattsburg and encamped just
outside the town.   From a ridge the British leader

beheld the redoubts, strong field works, and block-houses, and at anchor in the bay the little American fleet of Commodore Thomas Macdonough. To Prevost it looked like a costly business to attempt to carry these defenses by assault and he therefore decided to await the arrival of the British ships of Captain George Downie. A combined attack by land and sea, he believed, should find no difficulty in wiping out American resistance.

Such was the situation and the weighty responsibility which confronted Macdonough and his sailors. It was the most critical moment of the war. With a seaman's eye for defense Macdonough met it by stationing his vessels in a carefully chosen position and prepared with a seaman's foresight for every contingency. Plattsburg Bay is about two miles wide and two long and lies open to the southward, with a cape called Cumberland Head bounding it on the east. It was in this sheltered water that Macdonough awaited attack, his ships riding about a mile from the American shore batteries. These guns were to be captured by the British army and turned against him, according to the plans of General Prevost, who was urging Captain Downie to hasten with his fleet and undertake a joint action, for, as he said, "it is of the highest importance that the ships, vessels, and gunboats of your command should combine a coöperation with the division of the army under my command. I only wait for your arrival to proceed against General Macomb's last position on the south bank of the Saranac."

These demands became more and more insistent, although the largest British ship, the *Confiance*, had been launched only a few days before and the mechanics were still toiling night and day to fit her for action. She was a formidable frigate, of the size of the American *Chesapeake*, and was expected to be more than a match for Macdonough's entire fleet. Captain Downie certainly expected the support of the army, which he failed to receive, for he clearly stated his position before the naval battle. "When the batteries are stormed and taken possession of by the British land forces, which the commander of the land forces has promised to do at the moment the naval action commences, the enemy will be obliged to quit their position, whereby we shall obtain decided advantage over them during the confusion. I would otherwise prefer fighting them on the lake and would wait until our force is in an efficient state but I fear they would take shelter up the lake and would not meet me on equal terms."

Compelled to seek and offer battle in Plattsburg Bay, the British vessels rounded Cumberland
Head on the morning of the 11th of September and
hove to while Captain Downie went ahead in a
boat to observe the American position. He per-
ceived that Macdonough had anchored his fleet in
line in this order: the brig *Eagle*, twenty guns, the
flagship *Saratoga*, twenty-six guns, the schooner
Ticonderoga, seven guns, and the sloop *Preble*,
seven guns. There was also a considerable squadron of little gunboats, or galleys, propelled by oars
and mounting one gun. Opposed to this force was
the stately *Confiance*, with her three hundred men
and thirty-seven guns, such a ship as might have
dared to engage the *Constitution* on blue water,
and the *Chub*, *Linnet*, and *Finch*, much like Macdonough's three smaller vessels, besides a flotilla
of the tiny, impudent gunboats which were like
so many hornets.

Macdonough was a youngster of twenty-eight
years to whom was granted this opportunity denied
the officers who had grown gray in the service. The
navy, which was also very young, had set its own
stamp upon him, and his advancement he had
won by sheer ability. Self-reliant and indomitable,
like Oliver Hazard Perry, he had wrestled with

obstacles and was ready to meet the enemy in spite of them. His fame among naval men outshines Perry's, and he is rated as the greatest fighting sailor who flew the American flag until Farragut surpassed them all.

The battle of Plattsburg Bay was contested straight from the shoulder with little chance for such evolutions as seeking the weather gage or wearing ship. With one fleet at anchor, as Nelson demonstrated at the Nile, the proper business of the other was to drive ahead and try to break the line or turn an end of it. This Captain Downie proceeded to attempt in a brave and highly skillful manner, with the *Confiance* leading into the bay and proposing to smash the *Eagle* with her first broadsides. The wind failed, however, and the British frigate dropped anchor within close range of the *Saratoga*, which displayed Macdonough's pennant, and pounded this vessel so accurately that forty American seamen, or one-fifth of the crew, were struck down by the first blast of the British guns.

Meanwhile the *Linnet* had reached her assigned berth and fought the American *Eagle* so successfully that the latter was disabled and had to leave the line. To balance this the *Chub* was so badly damaged that she drifted helpless among the American ships and was compelled to haul down her colors. The *Finch* committed a blunder of seamanship and by failing to keep close enough to the wind, which soon died away, she finally went aground and took no part in the battle. The *Preble* was driven from her anchorage and ran ashore under the Plattsburg batteries, and the *Ticonderoga* played no heavier part than to beat off the little British galleys.

The decisive battle was therefore fought by four ships, the American *Saratoga* and *Eagle*, and the British *Confiance* and *Linnet*. It was then that Macdonough acquitted himself as a man who did not know when he was beaten. The *Confiance*, which must have towered like a ship of the line, had so cruelly mauled the *Saratoga* that she seemed doomed to be blown out of water. So many of his gunners were killed by the double-shotted broadsides that Macdonough jumped from the quarterdeck to take a hand himself and encourage the survivors. He was sighting a gun when a round shot cut the spanker boom, and a fragment of the heavy spar knocked him senseless.

Recovering his wits, however, he returned to his gun. But another shot tore off the head of the

gun captain and flung it in Macdonough's face
with such force that he was hurled across the deck.
At length all but one of the guns along the side
exposed to the *Confiance* had been smashed or dismounted, and this last gun broke its fastening
bolts, leaped from its carriage with the heavy recoil,
and plunged into the main hatch.   Silenced, shot
through and through, her decks strewn with dead,
the *Saratoga* might then have struck her colors with
honor.   But Macdonough had not begun to fight.
Prepared for such an emergency, he let go a stern
anchor, cut his bow cable, and "winded" or turned
his ship around so that her other side with its un-
injured row of guns was presented to the *Confiance*.
Captain Downie had by this time been killed, and
the acting commander of the British flagship endeavored to execute the same maneuver, but the
Confiance was too badly crippled to be swung about.
While she floundered, the Saratoga reduced her to
submission.   One of the surviving officers stated
that "the ship's company declared they would
no longer stand to their quarters nor could the
officers with their utmost exertions rally them."
The ship was sinking, with more than a hundred
ragged holes in her hull and fivescore men dead
or hurt.   Fifteen minutes later the plucky *Linnet*

surrendered after a long and desperate duel with
the *Eagle*. The British galleys escaped from the
bay under sail and oar because no American ships
were fit to chase them, but the Royal Navy had
ceased to exist on Lake Champlain. For more
than two hours the battle had been fought with
a bulldog endurance not often equaled in the grim
pages of naval history. And more nearly than
any other incident of the War of 1812 it could be
called decisive.

The American victory made the position of Prevost's army wholly untenable. With the control of
Lake Champlain in Macdonough's hands, the British line of communication would be continually
menaced. For the ten thousand veterans of Wellington's campaigns there was nothing to do but
retreat, nor did they linger until they had marched
across the Canada border. Though the way had
lain open before them, they had not fought a battle,
but were turned out of the United States, evicted,
one might say, by a few small ships manned by
several hundred American sailors. As Perry had
regained the vast Northwest for his nation so,
more momentously, did Macdonough avert from
New York and New England a tide of invasion
which could not otherwise have been stemmed.

CHAPTER X

PEACE WITH HONOR

THE raids of the British navy on the American sea-coast through the last two years of the war were so many efforts to make effective the blockade which began with the proclamation of December, 1812, closing Chesapeake and Delaware bays. Successive orders in 1813 closed practically all the seaports from New London, Connecticut, to the Florida boundary, and the last sweeping proclamation of May, 1814, placed under strict blockade "all the ports, harbors, bays, creeks, rivers, inlets, outlets, islands, and seacoasts of the United States." It was the blockade of ports of the Middle States which caused such widespread ruin among merchants and shippers and which finally brought the Government itself to the verge of bankruptcy.

The first serious alarm was caused in the spring of 1813 by the appearance of a British fleet, under command of Admiral Sir John Borlase Warren and

Rear-Admiral George Cockburn, in the Chesapeake and Delaware bays. Apparently it had not occurred to the people of the seaboard that the war might make life unpleasant for them, and they had undertaken no measures of defense. Unmolested, Cockburn cruised up Cheapeake Bay to the mouth of the Susquehanna in the spring of 1813 and established a pleasant camp on an island from which five hundred sailors and marines harried the country at their pleasure, looting and burning such prosperous little towns as Havre de Grace and Fredericktown. The men of Maryland and Virginia proceeded to hide their chattels and to move their families inland. Panic took hold of these proud and powerful commonwealths. Cockburn had no scruples about setting the torch to private houses, "to cause the proprietors who had deserted them and formed part of the militia which had fled to the woods to understand and feel what they were liable to bring upon themselves by building forts and acting toward us with so much useless rancor." Though Cockburn was an officer of the British navy, he was also an unmitigated ruffian in his behavior toward non-combatants, and his own countrymen could not regard his career with satisfaction.

Admiral Warren had more justification in attacking Norfolk, which had a navy yard and forts and was therefore frankly belligerent. Unluckily for him the most important battery was manned by a hundred sailors from the *Constellation* and fifty marines. Seven hundred British seamen tried to land in barges, but the battery shattered three of the boats with heavy loss of life. Somewhat ruffled, Admiral Warren decided to go elsewhere and made a foray upon the defenseless village of Hampton during which he permitted his men to indulge in wanton pillage and destruction. Part of his fleet then sailed up to the Potomac and created a most distressing hysteria in Washington. The movement was a feint, however, and after frightening Baltimore and Annapolis, the ships cruised and blockaded the bay for several months.

In September of the following year another British division harassed the coast of Maine, first capturing Eastport and then landing at Belfast, Bangor, and Castine, and extorting large ransoms in money and supplies. New England was wildly alarmed. In a few weeks all of Maine east of the Penobscot had been invaded, conquered, and formally annexed to New Brunswick, although two counties alone might easily have furnished twelve thousand fighting men to resist the small parties of British sailors who operated in leisurely security. The people of the coastwise towns gave up their sheep and bullocks to these rude trespassers, cut the corn and dug the potatoes for them, handed over all their powder and firearms, and agreed to finish and deliver schooners that were on the stocks.

Cape Cod was next to suffer, for two men-of-war levied contributions of thousands of dollars from Wellfleet, Brewster, and Eastham, and robbed and destroyed other towns. Farther south another fleet entered Long Island Sound, bombarded Stonington, and laid it in ruins. The pretext for all this havoc was a raid made by a few American troops who had crossed to Long Point on Lake Erie, May 15, 1814, and had burned some Canadian mills and a few dwellings. The expedition was promptly disowned by the American Government as unauthorized, but in retaliation the British navy was ordered to lay waste all towns on the Atlantic coast which were assailable, sparing only the lives of the unarmed citizens.

Included in the British plan of campaign for 1814 was a coastal attack important encugh to divert American efforts from the Canadian frontier. This was why an army under General Ross was

THOMAS MACDONOUGH

Painting by J. W. Jarvis. In the City Hall, New York, owned by the Corporation. Reproduced by courtesy of the Municipal Art Commission of the City of New York.

JACOB BROWN

Painting by J. W. Jarvis. In the City Hall, New York, owned by the Corporation. Reproduced by courtesy of the Municipal Art Commission of the City of New York.

THOMAS MACDONOUGH

Painting by J. W. Jarvis. In the City Hall, New York, owned by the Corporation. Reproduced by courtesy of the Municipal Art Commission of the City of New York.

JACOB BROWN

Painting by J. W. Jarvis. In the City Hall, New York, owned by the Corporation. Reproduced by courtesy of the Municipal Art Commission of the City of New York.

loaded into transports at Bermuda and escorted by a fleet to Chesapeake Bay. The raids against small coastwise ports, though lucrative, had no military value beyond shaking the morale of the population. The objective of this larger operation was undecided. Either Baltimore or Washington was tempting. But first the British had to dispose of the annoying gunboat flotilla of Commodore Joshua Barney, who had made his name mightily respected as a seaman of the Revolution and who had never been known to shake in his shoes at sight of a dozen British ensigns. He had found shelter for his armed scows, for they were no more than this, in the Patuxent River, but as he could not hope to defend them against a combined attack by British ships and troops he wisely blew them up.

This turn of affairs left a fine British army all landed and with nothing else to do than promenade through a pleasant region with nobody to interfere. The generals and admirals discussed the matter and decided to saunter on to Washington instead of to Baltimore. In the heat of August the British regiments tramped along the highways, frequently halting to rest in the shade, until they were within ten miles of the capital of the nation. There they found the American outposts in a strong position on high ground, but these tarried not, and the invaders sauntered on another mile before making camp for the night. It is difficult to regard the capture of Washington with the seriousness which that lamentable episode deserves. The city was greatly surprised to learn that the enemy actually intended a discourtesy so gross, and the Government was pained beyond expression. But beyond this display of emotion nothing was done. The war was now two years old but no steps whatever had been taken to defend Washington, although there was no room for doubt that a British naval force could ascend the river whenever it pleased.

The disagreeable tidings that fifty of the enemy's ships had anchored off the Potomac, however, reminded the President and his advisers that not a single ditch or rampart had been even planned, that no troops were at hand, that it was rather late for advice which seemed to be the only ammunition that was plentiful. Quite harmoniously, the soldier in command was General Winder who could not lose his head, even in this dire emergency, because he had none to lose. His record for ineptitude on the fighting front had, no doubt, recommended him for this place. He ran about Washington, ordering the construction of defenses which there was no time to build, listening to a million frenzied suggestions, holding all manner of consultations, and imploring the Governors of Pennsylvania, Maryland, and Virginia to send militia.

The British army was less than five thousand strong. To oppose them General Winder hastily scrambled together between five and six thousand men, mostly militia with a sprinkling of regulars and four hundred sailors from Barney's flotilla. During the night before the alleged battle the camp was a scene of such confusion as may be imagined while futile councils of war were held. The troops when reviewed by President Madison realized Jefferson's ideal of a citizen soldiery, unskilled but strong in their love of home, flying to arms to oppose an invader. General Jacob Brown and Winfield Scott at Lundy's Lane, which was fought within the same month, could have pointed out, in language quite emphatic, that a large difference existed between the raw material and the finished product.

On the 24th of August the British army advanced to Bladensburg, five miles from Washington, where a bridge spanned the eastern branch of the Potomac. Here the hilly banks offered the Americans an excellent line of defense. The

Cabinet had gone to the Washington Navy Yard, by request of General Winder, to tell him what he ought to do, but this final conference was cut short by the news that the enemy was in motion. The American forces were still mobilizing in helter-skelter fashion, and there was a wild race to the scene of action by militiamen, volunteers, unattached regulars, sailors, generals, citizens at large, Cabinet members, and President Madison himself.

Some Maryland militia hastily joined the Baltimore troops on the ridge behind the village of Bladensburg, but part of General Winder's own forces were still on the march and had not yet been assigned positions when the advance column of British light infantry were seen to rush down the slope across the river and charge straight for the bridge. They bothered not to seek a ford or to turn a flank but made straight for the American center. It was here that Winder's artillery and his steadiest regiments were placed and they offered a stiff resistance, ripping up the British vanguard with grapeshot and mowing men down right and left. But these hardened British campaigners had seen many worse days than this on the bloody fields of Spain, and they pushed forward, closing the gaps in their ranks, until they had crossed the bridge and could find a brief respite under cover of the trees which lined the stream. Advancing again, they ingeniously discharged flights of rockets and with these novel missiles they not only disorganized the militia in front of them but also stampeded the battery mules. Most of the American army promptly followed the mules and endeavored to set a new record for a foot race from Bladensburg to Washington. The Cabinet members and other dignified spectators were swept along in the rout.

Commodore Joshua Barney and his four hundred weather-beaten bluejackets declined to join this speed contest. They were used to rolling decks and had no aptitude for sprinting, besides which they held the simple-minded notion that their duty was to fight. Up to this time they had been held back by orders and now arrived just as the American lines broke in wild confusion. With them were five guns which they dragged into position across the main highway and speedily unlimbered. The British were hastening to overtake the fleeing enemy when they encountered this awkward obstacle. Three times they charged Barney's battery and were three times repulsed by sailors and marines who fought them with muskets, cutlasses,

13

and handspikes, and who served those five guns with an efficiency which would have pleased Isaac Hull or Bainbridge.

Unwilling to pay the price of direct attack, the British General Ross wisely ordered his infantry to surround Barney's stubborn contingent. The American troops who were presumed to support and protect this naval battery failed to hold their ground and melted into the mob which was swirling toward Washington. The sailors, though abandoned, continued to fight until the British were firing into them from the rear and from both flanks. Barney fell wounded and some of his gunners were bayoneted with lighted fuses in their hands. Snarling, undaunted, the sailors broke through the cordon and saved themselves, the last to leave a battlefield upon which not one American soldier was visible. They had used their ammunition to the end and they faced five thousand British veterans; wherefore they had done what the navy expected of them. On a day so shameful that no self-respecting American can read of it without blushing they had enacted the one redeeming episode. Commodore Barney described this action in a manner blunt and unadorned:

The engagement continued, the enemy advancing and our own army retreating before them, apparently in much disorder. At length the enemy made his appearance on the main road, in force, in front of my battery, and on seeing us made a halt. I reserved our fire. In a few minutes the enemy again advanced, when I ordered an eighteen-pounder to be fired, which completely cleared the road; shortly after, a second and a third attempt was made by the enemy to come forward but all were destroyed. They then crossed into an open field and attempted to flank our right. He was met there by three twelve-pounders, the marines under Captain Miller, and my men acting as infantry, and again was totally cut up. By this time not a vestige of the American army remained, except a body of five or six hundred posted on a height on my right, from which I expected much support from their fine situation.

Barney was made a prisoner, although his men stood by him until he ordered them to retreat. Loss of blood had made him too weak to be carried from the field. General Ross and Admiral Cockburn saw to it personally that he was well cared for and paid him the greatest respect and courtesy. As for the other British officers, they, too, were sportsmen who admired a brave man, even in the enemy's uniform, and Barney reported that they treated him "like a brother."

The American army had scampered to Washington with a total loss of ten killed and forty wounded among the five thousand men who had been assembled at Bladensburg to protect and save the capital. The British tried to pursue but the afternoon heat was blistering and the rapid pace set by the American forces proved so fatiguing to the invaders that many of them were bowled over by sunstroke. To permit their men to run themselves to death did not appear sensible to the British commanders, and they therefore sat down to gain their breath before the final promenade to Washington in the cool of the evening. They found a helpless, almost deserted city from which the Government had fled and the army had vanished.

The march had been orderly, with a proper regard for the peaceful inhabitants, but now Ross and Cockburn carried out their orders to plunder and burn. At the head of their troops they rode to the Capitol, fired a volley through the windows, and set fire to the building. Two hundred men then sought the President's mansion, ransacked the rooms, and left it in flames. Next day they burned the official buildings and several dwellings and, content with the mischief thus wrought, abandoned the forlorn city and returned to camp at

Bladensburg. But more vexation for the Americans was to follow, for a British fleet was working its way up the Potomac to anchor off Alexandria. Here there was the same frightened submission, with the people asking for terms and yielding up a hundred thousand dollars' worth of flour, tobacco, naval stores, and shipping.

The British squadron then returned to Chesapeake Bay and joined the main fleet which was preparing to attack Baltimore. The army of General Ross was recalled to the transports and was set ashore at the mouth of the Patapsco River while the ships sailed up to bombard Fort McHenry, where the star-spangled banner waved. To defend Baltimore by land there had been assembled more than thirteen thousand troops under command of General Samuel Smith. The tragical farce of Bladensburg, however, had taught him no lesson, and to oppose the five thousand toughened regulars of General Ross he sent out only three thousand green militia most of whom had never been under fire. They put up a wonderfully good fight and deserved praise for it, but wretched leadership left them drawn up in an open field, with both flanks unprotected, and they were soon driven back. Next morning — the 13th of September — the British advanced but found the roads so blocked by fallen trees and entanglements that progress was slow and laborious. The intrenchments which crowned the hills of Baltimore appeared so formidable that the British decided to await action by the fleet and attempt a night assault.

General Ross was killed during the advance, and this loss caused confusion of council. The heavy ships were unable to lie within effective range of the forts because of shoal water and a barrier of sunken hulks, and Fort McHenry was almost undamaged by the bombardment of the lighter craft. All through the night a determined fire was returned by the American garrison of a thousand men, and, although the British fleet suffered little, Vice-Admiral Cochrane concluded that a sea attack was a hopeless enterprise. He so notified the army, which thereupon retreated to the transports, and the fleet sailed down Chesapeake Bay, leaving Baltimore free and unscathed.

Among those who watched Fort McHenry by the glare of artillery fire through this anxious night was a young lawyer from Washington, Francis Scott Key, who had been detained by the British fleet down the bay while endeavoring to effect an exchange of prisoners. He had a turn for verse-making. Most of his poems were mediocre, but the sight of the Stars and Stripes still fluttering in the early morning breeze inspired him to write certain deathless stanzas which, when fitted to the old tune of *Anacreon in Heaven,* his country accepted as its national anthem. In this exalted moment it was vouchsafed him to sound a trumpet call, clear and far-echoing, as did Rouget de Lisle when, with soul aflame, he wrote the *Marseillaise* for France. If it was the destiny of the War of 1812 to weld the nation as a union, the spirit of the consummation was expressed for all time in the lines which a hundred million of free people sing today:

O! say can you see by the dawn's early light,
　　What so proudly we hail'd at the twilight's last
　　　　gleaming
Whose broad stripes and bright stars through the
　　　　perilous fight,
　　O'er the ramparts we watch'd, were so gallantly
　　　　streaming?

The luckless endeavor to capture Baltimore by sea and land was the last British expedition that alarmed the Atlantic coast. The hostile army and naval forces withdrew to Jamaica, from which base were planned and undertaken the Louisiana campaign and the battle of New Orleans.

The brilliant leadership and operations of Andrew Jackson were so detached and remote from all other activities that he may be said to have fought a private war of his own. It had seemed clear to Madison that, as a military precaution, the control of West Florida should be wrenched from Spain, whose neutrality was dubious and whose Gulf territory was the rendezvous of privateers, pirates, and other lawless gentry, besides offering convenient opportunity for British invasion by sea. As early as the autumn of 1812 troops were collected to seize and hold this region for the duration of the war. The people of the Mississippi Valley welcomed the adventure with enthusiasm. It was to be aimed against a European power presumably friendly, but the sheer love of conquest and old grudges to settle were motives which brushed argument aside. Andrew Jackson was the major general of the Tennessee militia, and so many hardy volunteers flocked to follow him that he had to sift them out, mustering in at Nashville two thousand of whom he said: "They are the choicest of our citizens. They go at our call to do the will of

Government. No constitutional scruples trouble them. Nay, they will rejoice at the opportunity of placing the American eagle on the ramparts of Pensacola, Mobile, and Fort St. Augustine."

Where the fiery Andrew Jackson led, there was neither delay nor hesitation. At once he sent his backwoods infantry down river in boats, while the mounted men rode overland. Four weeks later the information overtook him at Natchez that Congress had refused to sanction the expedition. When the Secretary of War curtly told him that his corps was "dismissed from public service," Andrew Jackson in a furious temper ignored the order and marched his men back to Nashville instead of disbanding them. He was not long idle, however, for the powerful confederacy of the Creek Indians had been aroused by a visit of the great Tecumseh, and the drums of the war dance were sounding in sympathy with the tribes of the Canadian frontier. In Georgia and Alabama the painted prophets and medicine men were spreading tales of Indian victories over the white men at the river Raisin and Detroit. British officials, moreover, got wind of a threatened uprising in the South and secretly encouraged it.

The Alabama settlers took alarm and left their

log houses and clearings to seek shelter in the nearest blockhouses and stockades. One of these belonged to Samuel Mims, a half-breed farmer, who had prudently fortified his farm on a bend of the Alabama River. A square stockade enclosed an acre of ground around his house and to this refuge hastened several hundred pioneers and their families, with their negro slaves, and a few officers and soldiers. Here they were surprised and massacred by a thousand naked Indians who called themselves Red Sticks because of the wands carried by their fanatical prophets. Two hundred and fifty scalps were carried away on poles, and when troops arrived they found nothing but heaps of ashes, mutilated bodies, and buzzards feeding on the carrion.

From Fort Mims the Indians overran the country like a frightful scourge, murdering and burning, until a vast region was emptied of its people. First to respond to the pitiful calls for help was Tennessee, and within a few weeks twenty-five hundred infantry and a thousand cavalry were marching into Alabama, led by Andrew Jackson, who had not yet recovered from a wound received in a brawl with Thomas H. Benton. Among Jackson's soldiers were two young men after his own heart, David Crockett and Samuel Houston.   The

villages of the fighting Creeks, at the Hickory
Ground, lay beyond a hundred and sixty miles of
wilderness, but Jackson would not wait for supplies. He plunged ahead, living somehow on the
country, until his men, beginning to break under
the strain of starvation and other hardships, declared open mutiny. But Jackson cursed, threatened, argued them into obedience again and again.
When such persuasions failed, he planted cannon to
sweep their lines and told them they would have to
pass over his dead body if they refused to go on.

The failure of other bodies of troops to support
his movements and a discouraged Governor of
Tennessee could not daunt his purpose. He was
told that the campaign had failed and that the
struggle was useless. To this he replied that he
would perish first and that energy and decision,
together with the fresh troops promised him, would
solve the crisis. Months passed, and the militia
whose enlistments had expired went home, while
the other broke out in renewed and more serious
mutinies. The few regulars sent to Jackson he
used as police to keep the militia in order. The
court-martialing and shooting of a private had a
beneficial effect.

With this disgruntled, unreliable, weary force,

Jackson came, at length, to a great war camp of the Creek Indians at a loop of the Tallapoosa River called Horsehoe Bend. Here some ten hundred picked warriors had built defensive works which were worthy of the talent of a trained engineer. They also had as effective firearms as the white troops who assaulted the stronghold. Andrew Jackson bombarded them with two light guns, sent his men over the breastworks, and captured the breastworks in hand-to-hand fighting in which quarter was neither asked nor given. No more than a hundred Indians escaped alive, and dead among the logs and brushwood were the three famous prophets, gorgeous in war paint and feathers, who had preached the doctrine of exterminating the paleface.

The name of Andrew Jackson spread far and wide among the hostile Indian tribes, and the fiercest chiefs dreaded it like a tempest. Some made submission, and others joined in signing a treaty of peace which Jackson dictated to them with terms as harsh as the temper of the man who had conquered them.

For his distinguished services Jackson was made a major general of the regular army. He was then ordered to Mobile, where his impetuous anger was aroused by the news that the British had landed at

Pensacola and had pulled down the Spanish flag. The splendor of this ancient seaport had passed away, and with it the fleets of galleons whose sailors heard the mission bells and saw the brass guns gleam from the stout fortresses which in those earlier days guarded the rich commerce of the overland trade route to St. Augustine.

Aforetime one of the storied and romantic ports of the Spanish Main, Pensacola now slumbered in unlovely decay and was no more than a village to which resorted the smugglers of the Caribbean, the pirates of the Gulf, and rascally men of all races and colors. The Spanish Governor still lived in the palace with a few slovenly troops, but he could no more than protest when a hundred royal marines came ashore from two British sloops-of-war, and the commander, Major Nicholls, issued a thunderous proclamation to the oppressed people of the American States adjoining, letting them know that he was ready to assist them in liberating their paternal soil from a faithless, imbecile Government. They were not to be alarmed at his approach. They were to range themselves under the standard of their forefathers or be neutral.

Having fired this verbal blunderbuss, Major Nicholls sent a sloop-of-war to enlist the support of

Jean and Pierre Lafitte, enterprising brothers who maintained on Barataria Bay in the Gulf, some forty miles south of New Orleans, a most lucrative resort for pirates and slave traders. There they defied the law and the devil, trafficking in spoils filched from honest merchantmen whose crews had walked the plank. Pierre Lafitte was a very proper figure of a pirate himself, true to the best traditions of his calling. But withal he displayed certain gallantry to atone for his villainies, for he spurned British gold and persuasions and offered his sword and his men to defend New Orleans as one faithful to the American cause.

If it was the purpose of Nicholls to divert Jackson's attention from New Orleans which was to be the objective of the British expedition preparing at Jamaica, he succeeded admirably; but in deciding to attack Jackson's forces at Mobile, he committed a grievous error. The worthy Nicholls failed to realize that he had caught a Tartar in General Jackson — "Old Hickory," the sinewy backwoodsman who would sooner fight than eat and who was feared more than the enemy by his own men. As might have been expected, the garrison of one hundred and sixty soldiers who held Fort Bowyer, which dominated the harbor of

Mobile, solemnly swore among themselves that they would never surrender until the ramparts were demolished over their heads and no more than a corporal's guard survived. This was Andrew Jackson's way.

Four British ships, with a total strength of seventy-eight guns, sailed into Mobile Bay on the 15th of September and formed in line of battle, easily confident of smashing Fort Bowyer with its twenty guns, while the landing force of marines and Indians took position behind the sand dunes and awaited the signal. The affair lasted no more than an hour. The American gunnery overwhelmed the British squadron. The *Hermes* sloop-of-war was forced to cut her cable and drifted under a raking fire until she ran aground and was blown up. The *Sophie* withdrew after losing many of her seamen, and the two other ships followed her to sea after delaying to pick up the marines and Indians who merely looked on. Daybreak saw the squadron spreading topsails to return to Pensacola.

Andrew Jackson was eager to return the compliment but, not having troops enough at hand to march on Pensacola, he had to wait and fret until his force was increased to four thousand men. Then he hurled them at the objective with an energy that was fairly astounding. On the 3d of November he left Mobile and three days later was demanding the surrender of Pensacola. The next morning he carried the town by storm, waited another day until the British had evacuated and blown up Fort Barrancas, six miles below the city, and then returned to Mobile. Sickness laid him low but, enfeebled as he was, he made the journey to New Orleans by easy stages and took command of such American troops as he could hastily assemble to ward off the mightiest assault launched by Great Britain during the War of 1812. It was known, and the warning had been repeated from Washington, that the enemy intended sending a formidable expedition against Louisiana, but when Jackson arrived early in December the Legislature had voted no money, raised no regiments, devised no plan of defense, and was unprepared to make any resistance whatever.

A British fleet of about fifty sail, carrying perhaps a thousand guns, had gathered for the task in hand. The decks were crowded with trained and toughened troops, the divisions which had scattered the Americans at Bladensburg with a volley and a shout, kilted Highlanders, famous regiments which had earned the praise of the Iron Duke in the

Spanish Peninsula, and brawny negro detachments recruited in the West Indies. It was such an army as would have been considered fit to withstand the finest troops in Europe. In command was one of England's most brilliant soldiers, General Sir Edward Pakenham, of whom Wellington had said, "my partiality for him does not lead me astray when I tell you that he is one of the best we have." He was the idol of his officers, who agreed that they had never served under a man whose good opinion they were so desirous of having, "and to fall in his estimation would have been worse than death." In brief, he was a high-minded and knightly leader who had seen twenty years of active service in the most important campaigns of Europe.

It was Pakenham's misfortune to be unacquainted with the highly irregular and unconventional methods of warfare as practiced in America, where troops preferred to take shelter instead of being shot down while parading across open ground in solid columns. Improvised breastworks were to him a novelty, and the lesson of Bunker Hill had been forgotten. These splendidly organized and seasoned battalions of his were confident of walking through the Americans at New Orleans as they had done at Washington, or as Pakenham himself

14

had smashed the finest French infantry at Salamanca when Wellington told him, "Ned, d'ye see those fellows on the hill? Throw your division into column; at them, and drive them to the devil."

Stranger than fiction was the contrast between the leaders and between the armies that fought this extraordinary battle of New Orleans when, after the declaration of peace, the United States won its one famous but belated victory on land. On the northern frontier such a man as Andrew Jackson might have changed the whole aspect of the war. He was a great general with the rare attribute of reading correctly the mind of an opponent and divining his course of action, endowed with an unyielding temper and an iron hand, a relentless purpose, and the faculty of inspiring troops to follow, obey, and trust him in the last extremity. He was one of them, typifying their passions and prejudices, their faults and their virtues, sharing their hardships as if he were a common private, never grudging them the credit in success.

In the light of previous events it is probable that any other American general would have felt justified in abandoning New Orleans without a contest. In the city itself were only eight hundred regulars newly recruited and a thousand volunteers. But

Jackson counted on the arrival of the hard-bitted, Indian-fighting regiments of Tennessee who were toiling through the swamps with their brigadiers, Coffee and Carroll.   The foremost of them reached New Orleans on the very day that the British were landing on the river bank.   Gaunt, unshorn, untamed were these rough-and-tumble warriors who feared neither God nor man but were glad to fight and die with Andrew Jackson.   In coonskin caps, buckskin shirts, fringed leggings, they swaggered into New Orleans, defiant of discipline and impatient of restraint, hunting knives in their belts, long rifles upon their shoulders.   There they drank with seamen as wild as themselves who served in the ships of Jackson's small naval force or had offered to lend a hand behind the stockades, and with lean, long-legged Yankees from down East, swarthy outlaws who sailed for Pierre Lafitte, Portuguese and Norwegian wanderers who had deserted their merchant vessels, and even Spanish adventurers from the West Indies.

The British fleet disembarked its army late in December after the most laborious difficulties because of the many miles of shallow bayou and toilsome marsh which delayed the advance.   A week was required to carry seven thousand men in small boats from the ships to the Isle aux Poix on Lake Borgne chosen as a landing base. Thence a brigade passed in boats up the bayou and on the 23d of December disembarked at a point some three miles from the Mississippi and then by land and canal pushed on to the river's edge. Here they were attacked at night by Jackson with about two thousand troops, while a war schooner shelled the British left from the river. It was a weird fight. Squads of Grenadiers, Highlanders, Creoles, and Tennessee backwoodsmen blindly fought each other in the fog with knives, fists, bayonets, and musket butts. Jackson then fell back while the British brigade waited for more troops and artillery.

On Christmas Day Pakenham took command of the forces at the front now augmented to about six thousand, but hesitated to attack. And well he might hesitate, in spite of his superior numbers, for Jackson had employed his time well and now lay entrenched behind a parapet, protected by a canal or ditch ten feet wide. With infinite exertion more guns were dragged and floated to the front until eight heavy batteries were in position. On the morning of the 1st of January the British gunners opened fire and felt serenely certain of destroying the rude defenses of cotton bales and cypress logs. To their amazement the American artillery was served with far greater precision and effect by the sailors and regulars who had been trained under Jackson's direction. By noon most of the British guns had been silenced or dismounted and the men killed or driven away. "Never was any failure more remarkable or unlooked for than this," said one of the British artillery officers. General Pakenham, in dismay, held a council of war. It is stated that his own judgment was swayed by the autocratic Vice-Admiral Cochrane who tauntingly remarked that "if the army could not take those mud-banks, defended by ragged militia, he would undertake to do it with two thousand sailors armed only with cutlases and pistols."

Made cautious by this overwhelming artillery reverse, the British army remained a week in camp, a respite of which every hour was priceless to Andrew Jackson, for his mud-stained, haggard men were toiling with pick and shovel to complete the ditches and log barricades. They could hear the British drums and bugles echo in the gloomy cypress woods while the cannon grumbled incessantly. The red-coated sentries were stalked and the pickets were ambushed by the Indian fighters who

spread alarm and uneasiness.   Meanwhile Pakenham was making ready with every resource known
to picked troops, who had charged unshaken
through the slaughter of Ciudad Rodrigo, Badajoz,
and San Sebastian, and who were about to justify
once more the tribute to the British soldier: "Give
him a plain, unconditional order — go and do *that*
— and he will do it with a cool, self-forgetting per-
tinacity that can scarcely be too much admired."

It was Pakenham's plan to hurl a flank attack
against the right bank of the Mississippi while he
directed the grand assault on the east side of the
river where Jackson's strength was massed.   To
protect the flank, Commodore Patterson of the
American naval force had built a water battery of
nine guns and was supported by eight hundred
militia.   Early in the morning of the 8th of January twelve hundred men in boats, under the British
Colonel Thornton, set out to take this west bank
as the opening maneuver of the battle.   Their
errand was delayed, although later in the day they
succeeded in defeating the militia and capturing
the naval guns.   This minor victory, however, was
too late to save Pakenham's army which had been
cut to pieces in the frontal assault.

Jackson had arranged his main body of troops

along the inner edge of the small canal extending from a levee to a tangled swamp. The legendary cotton bales had been blown up or set on fire during the artillery bombardment and protection was furnished only by a raw, unfinished parapet of earth and a double row of log breastworks with red clay tamped between them. It was a motley army that Jackson led. Next to the levee were posted a small regiment of regular infantry, a company of New Orleans Rifles, a squad of dragoons who were handling a howitzer, and a battalion of Creoles in bright uniforms. The line was extended by the freebooters of Pierre Lafitte, their heads bound with crimson kerchiefs, a group of American bluejackets, a battalion of blacks from San Domingo, a few grizzled old French soldiers serving a brass gun, long rows of tanned, saturnine Tennesseans, more regulars with a culverin, and rank upon rank of homespun hunting shirts and long rifles, John Adair and his savage Kentuckians, and, knee-deep in the swamp, the frontiersmen who followed General Coffee to death or glory.

A spirit of reckless elation pervaded this bizarre and terrible little army, although it was well aware that during two and a half years almost every other American force had been defeated by an enemy far less formidable. The anxious faces were those of the men of Louisiana who fought for hearth and home, with their backs to the wall. Many a brutal tale had they heard of these war-hardened British veterans whose excesses in Portugal were notorious and who had laid waste the harmless hamlets of Maryland. All night Andrew Jackson's defenders stood on the *qui vive* until the morning mist of the 8th of January was dispelled and the sunlight flashed on the solid ranks of British bayonets no more than four hundred yards away.

At the signal rocket the enemy swept forward toward the canal, with companies of British sappers bearing scaling ladders and fascines of sugar cane. They moved with stolid unconcern, but the American cannon burst forth and slew them until the ditch ran red with blood. With cheers the invincible British infantry tossed aside its heavy knapsacks, scrambled over the ditch, and broke into a run to reach the earthworks along which flamed the sparse line of American rifles. Against such marksmen as these there was to be no work with the bayonet, for the assaulting column literally fell as falls the grass under the keen scythe. The survivors retired, however, only to join a fresh attack which was rallied and led by Pakenham himself.

He died with his men, but once more British pluck attempted the impossible, and the Highland brigade was chosen to lead this forlorn hope. That night the pipers wailed *Lochaber no more* for the mangled dead of the MacGregors, the MacLeans, and the MacDonalds who lay in windrows with their faces to the foe. This was no Bladensburg holiday, and the despised Americans were paying off many an old score. Two thousand of the flower of Britain's armies were killed or wounded in the few minutes during which the two assaults were so rashly attempted in parade formation. Coolly, as though at a prize turkey shoot on a tavern green, the American riflemen fired into these masses of doomed men, and every bullet found its billet.

On the right of the line a gallant British onslaught led by Colonel Rennie swept over a redoubt and the American defenders died to a man. But the British wave was halted and rolled back by a tempest of bullets from the line beyond, and the broken remnant joined the general retreat which was sounded by the British trumpeters. An armistice was granted next day and in shallow trenches the dead were buried, row on row, while the muffled drums rolled in honor of three generals, seven colonels, and seventy-five other officers who had died with their men. Behind the log walls and earthworks loafed the unkempt, hilarious heroes of whom only seventy-one had been killed or hurt, and no more than thirteen of these in the grand assault which Pakenham had led. "Old Hickory" had told them that they could lick their weight in wildcats, and they were ready to agree with him.

Magnificent but useless, after all, excepting as a proud heritage for later generations and a vindication of American valor against odds, was this battle of New Orleans which was fought while the Salem ship, *Astrea*, Captain John Derby, was driving home to the westward with the news that a treaty of peace had been signed at Ghent. With a sense of mutual relief the United States and England had concluded a war in which neither nation had definitely achieved its aims. The treaty failed to mention such vital issues as the impressment of seamen and the injury to commerce by means of paper blockades, while on the other hand England relinquished its conquest of the Maine coast and its claim to military domination of the Great Lakes. English statesmen were heartily tired of a war in which they could see neither profit nor glory, and even the Duke of Wellington had announced it as his opinion "that no military advantage can be expected if the war goes on, and I would have great reluctance in undertaking the command unless we made a serious effort first to obtain peace without insisting upon keeping any part of our conquests." The reverses of first-class British armies at Plattsburg, Baltimore, and New Orleans had been a bitter blow to English pride. Moreover, British commerce on the seas had been largely destroyed by a host of Yankee privateers, and the common people in England were suffering from scarcity of food and raw materials and from high prices to a degree comparable with the distress inflicted by the German submarine campaign a century later. And although the terms of peace were unsatisfactory to many Americans, it was implied and understood that the flag and the nation had won a respect and recognition which should prevent a recurrence of such wrongs as had caused the War of 1812. One of the Peace Commissioners, Albert Gallatin, a man of large experience, unquestioned patriotism, and lucid intelligence, set it down as his deliberate verdict:

The war has been productive of evil and of good, but I think the good preponderates. Independent of the loss of lives, and of the property of individuals, the war has laid the foundation of permanent taxes and military establishments which the Republicans had deemed unfavorable to the happiness and free institutions of our country. But under our former system we were becoming too selfish, too much attached exclusively to the acquisition of wealth, above all, too much confined in our political feelings to local and state objects. The war has renewed and reinstated the national feeling and character which the Revolution had given, and which were daily lessening. The people have now more general objects of attachment, with which their pride and political opinions are connected. They are more Americans; they feel and act more as a nation; and I hope that the permanency of the Union is thereby better secured.

After a hundred years, during which this peace was unbroken, a commander of the American navy, speaking at a banquet in the ancient Guildhall of London, was bold enough to predict: "If the time ever comes when the British Empire is seriously menaced by an external enemy, it is my opinion that you may count upon every man, every dollar, and every drop of blood of your kindred across the sea."

The prediction came true in 1917, and traditional enmities were extinguished in the crusade against a mutual and detestable foe. The candid naval officer became Vice-Admiral William S. Sims, commanding all the American ships and sailors in European waters, where the Stars and Stripes and the British ensign flew side by side, and the squadrons toiled and dared together in the finest spirit of admiration and respect.   Out from Queenstown sailed an American destroyer flotilla operated by a stern, inflexible British admiral who was never known to waste a compliment.   At the end of the first year's service he said to the officers of these hard-driven vessels:

I wish to express my deep gratitude to the United States officers and ratings for the skill, energy, and unfailing good nature which they have all so consistently shown and which qualities have so materially assisted in the war by enabling ships of the Allied Powers to cross the ocean in comparative freedom.

To command you is an honor, to work with you is a pleasure, to know you is to know the finest traits of the Anglo-Saxon race.

The United States waged a just war in 1812 and vindicated the principles for which she fought, but as long as the poppies blow in Flanders fields it is the clear duty, and it should be the abiding pleasure, of her people to remember, not those far-off days as foemen, but these latter days as comrades in arms.

BIBLIOGRAPHICAL NOTE

OF the scores of books that have been written about the War of 1812, many deal with particular phases, events, or personalities, and most of them are biased by partisan feeling. This has been unfortunately true of the textbooks written for American schools, which, by ignoring defeats and blunders, have missed the opportunity to teach the lessons of experience. By all odds the best, the fairest, and the most complete narrative of the war as written by an American historian is the monumental work of Henry Adams, *History of the United States of America*, 9 vols. (1889–91). The result of years of scholarly research, it is also most excellent reading.

Captain Mahan's *Sea Power in its Relation to the War of 1812*, 2 vols. (1905), is, of course, the final word concerning the naval events, but he also describes with keen analysis the progress of the operations on land and fills in the political background of cause and effect. Theodore Roosevelt's *The Naval War of 1812* (1882) is spirited and accurate but makes no pretensions to a general survey. Akin to such a briny book as this but more restricted in scope is *The Frigate Constitution* (1900) by Ira N. Hollis, or Rodney Macdonough's *Life of Commodore Thomas Macdonough* (1909). Edgar Stanton Maclay in *The History of the Navy*, 3 vols.

(1902), has written a most satisfactory account, which contains some capital chapters describing the immortal actions of the Yankee frigates.

Benson J. Lossing's *The Pictorial Field Book of the War of 1812* (1868) has enjoyed wide popularity because of his gossipy, entertaining quality. The author gathered much of his material at first hand and had the knack of telling a story; but he is not very trustworthy.

As a solemn warning, the disasters of the American armies have been employed by several military experts. The ablest of these was Bvt. Major General Emory Upton, whose invaluable treatise, *The Military Policy of the United States* (1904), was pigeonholed in manuscript by the War Department and allowed to gather dust for many years. He discusses in detail the misfortunes of 1812 as conclusive proof that the national defense cannot be entrusted to raw militia and untrained officers. Of a similar trend but much more recent are Frederic L. Huidekoper's *The Military Unpreparedness of the United States* (1915) and Major General Leonard Wood's *Our Military History; Its Facts and Fallacies* (1916).

Of the British historians, William James undertook the most diligent account of them all, calling it *A Full and Correct Account of the Military Occurrences of the Late War between Great Britain and the United States of America*, 2 vols. (1818). It is irritating reading for an American because of an enmity so bitter that facts are willfully distorted and glaring inaccuracies are accepted as truth. As a naval historian James undertook to explain away the American victories in single-ship actions, a difficult task in which he acquitted himself with poor grace. Theodore Roosevelt is at his best when he chastises James for his venomous hatred of all things American.

To the English mind the War of 1812 was only an episode in the mighty and prolonged struggle against Napoleon, and therefore it finds but cursory treatment in the standard English histories. To Canada, however, the conflict was intimate and vital, and the narratives written from this point of view are sounder and of more moment than those produced across the water. *The Canadian War of 1812* (1906), published almost a century after the event, is the work of an Englishman, Sir Charles P. Lucas, whose lifelong service in the Colonial Office and whose thorough acquaintance with Canadian history have both been turned to the best account. Among the Canadian authors in this field are Colonel Ernest A. Cruikshank and James Hannay. To Colonel Cruikshank falls the greater credit as a pioneer with his *Documentary History of the Campaign upon the Niagara Frontier*, 8 vols. (1896–). Hannay's *How Canada Was Held for the Empire; The Story of the War of 1812* (1905) displays careful study but is marred by the controversial and one-sided attitude which this war inspired on both sides of the border.

Colonel William Wood has avoided this flaw in his *War with the United States* (1915) which was published as a volume of the *Chronicles of Canada* series. As a compact and scholarly survey, this little book is recommended to Americans who comprehend that there are two sides to every question. The Canadians fought stubbornly and successfully to defend their country against invasion in a war whose slogan "Free Trade and Sailors' Rights" was no direct concern of theirs.

15

INDEX